Susan B. Carrafiello

"The Tombs of the Living"

Prisons and Prison Reform in Liberal Italy

PETER LANG
New York • Washington, D.C./Baltimore • Boston
Bern • Frankfurt am Main • Berlin • Vienna • Paris

Library of Congress Cataloging-in-Publication Data

Carrafiello, Susan B.
"The tombs of the living": prisons and prison
reform in liberal Italy / Susan B. Carrafiello.
p. cm. — (Studies in modern European history; 24)
Includes bibliographical references.
1. Prisons—Italy—History. 2. Prison reformers—Italy—History.
3. Italy—Politics and government—1870–1915. I. Title. II. Series:
Studies in modern European history; vol. 24.
HV9689.C375   365'.945—dc21   97-8537
ISBN 0-8204-3778-6
ISSN 0893-6897

Die Deutsche Bibliothek-CIP-Einheitsaufnahme

Carrafiello, Susan B.:
"The tombs of the living": prisons and prison
reform in liberal Italy / Susan B. Carrafiello. –New York;
Washington, D.C./Baltimore; Boston; Bern;
Frankfurt am Main; Berlin; Vienna; Paris: Lang.
(Studies in modern European history; Vol. 24)
ISBN 0-8204-3778-6 Gb.

Cover design by James F. Brisson.

The paper in this book meets the guidelines for permanence and durability
of the Committee on Production Guidelines for Book Longevity
of the Council of Library Resources.

Table of Contents

Acknowledgments

An author has many debts to acknowledge. I must first thank my graduate adviser, Charles F. Delzell, who supervised the thesis that served as the foundation of this book. Generous grants from Vanderbilt University and Wright State University made completion of this project possible. I also wish to thank the authorities and staff of the Archivio Centrale dello Stato in Rome for their helpful assistance during my research trips to Italy. My colleagues in the history department of Wright State University have provided kind encouragement.

On a more personal level, I wish to thank my parents, Richard and Betty Benton, for raising me with a sense of responsibility and intellectual curiosity. My husband and fellow historian, Michael L. Carrafiello, was an enthusiastic and helpful assistant in the final preparation of this volume. Finally, I recognize my son, Joey, for the joy he brings to all parts of my life.

1

Introduction

This study examines prison reform, and especially the idea of the penitentiary, in Italy in the nineteenth and early twentieth centuries. Its first goal is to examine the theories of prison reform developed by Italian intellectuals, politicians, and prison reformers before and after national unification in 1861. Its second aim is to calculate how effectively these ideas were realized and implemented in Italy, especially during the liberal era, 1861–1915. Lastly, it seeks to explain what Italy's success or failure in prison reform reveals about the Italian state after unification.

The penitentiary has captured the attention of recent historians. For many years, the development of the penitentiary was seen as the humanitarian invention of enlightened reformers who sought to substitute the humane and hygienic penitentiary for torture and the death penalty. An American historian, David Rothman, first questioned these motives in his pioneering effort, *The Discovery of the Asylum* (1971). In this work, he argued that both the asylum and the penitentiary emerged when traditional mores and values began to shift in Jacksonian America. These new institutions were offered as a means of stabilizing and controlling society.

The work of Michel Foucault has been even more influential in altering the interpretation of the penitentiary. In *Discipline and Punish* (1975), Foucault explored the transformation of punishment in the late-eighteenth and early nineteenth centuries. But he was not just interested in punishment. As David Garland has pointed out, Foucault saw the study of the prison as "a means of exploring the much wider (and more contemporary) theme of how domination is achieved and individuals are socially constructed in the modern world."[1] Foucault thus argued that the prison was just one of many "carcerals" that emerged simultaneously with the development of modern industrial society. These "carcerals," which included the school, the asylum, and even the hospital, were designed to create a disciplinary society in which individuals conformed and obeyed the dominant power. They were thus means to discipline and control modern society and marginalize all "deviants."

Foucault's particular historical concern was to explain the reason why punishment moved out of the public theater of the piazza into the enclosed cellular penitentiary. According to Foucault, the idea of the penitentiary did not develop as a humanitarian response to torture but rather because of fundamental changes in the nature of crime and criminal activity. In particular, the increase in crimes of property compelled the transformation of criminal justice. Indeed, Foucault argued that the prison emerged in spite of the reformers' pleas that punishment should remain visible to the public. The prison disciplined the body of the criminal in time and space, keeping him under constant surveillance. For Foucault, Jeremy Bentham's Panopticon symbolized the penitentiary ideal.

Foucault asserted that the prison failed in its attempts to discipline the prisoners. He maintained that the earliest reformers recognized the fundamental flaws in the prison, including its failure to deter crime and its promotion of criminal behavior. But this failure, he argued, was an essential aspect of the prison and prison reform because it helped to create a class of criminals. These people then served, among other things, to help control the working class and to enrich the dominant power. The prison, like the other "carcerals," was thus a disciplinary mechanism rather than a means of correcting offenders.[2]

The ideas of both Rothman and Foucault informed the work of several other historians. Patricia O'Brien, for example, in *The Promise of Punishment: Prisons in Nineteenth-Century France* (1982), examined the development of French prisons and the inmates that inhabited them. She argued that the interrelationship between the prison as an institution in French society and the simultaneous development of inmate subcultures help explain changes in the style of punishment in nineteenth-century France. In *A Just Measure of Pain: The Penitentiary in the Industrial Revolution, 1750–1850* (1978), Michael Ignatieff traced the transformation of the English system of punishment in the context of the Industrial Revolution. He considered the disciplinary technique of the penitentiary as an instrument of social control rather than a humanitarian effort by early English reformers. He argued that the prisoners' "right to decent treatment remained conditional on their willingness to reenter the moral consensus." Like Foucault, he maintained that "It was no accident that penitentiaries, asylums, workhouses . . . looked alike, or that their charges marched to the same disciplinary cadence." These institutions together "made up a complementary and interdependent structure of control."[3]

In a subsequent article, Ignatieff established the links between his ideas and the work of Foucault and David Rothman. But he also acknowledged that this "revisionist" interpretation of the development and purpose of the penitentiary has been somewhat undermined by recent historical scholarship. Gordon Wright, for example, called for a return to the "older orthodoxy" and contended that the penitentiary was in fact the invention of the largely humanitarian impulses of the Enlightenment.[4] Another important postrevisionist school of thought, meanwhile, stressed the incomplete nature of the "revolution in discipline." Margaret DeLacy's work, *Prison Reform in Lancashire, 1750–1840* (1986), revealed that the English county of Lancashire failed to complete a comprehensive reform of the prison system because of a shortage of money. So, too, Michelle Perrot and Jacques Leonard maintained in *L'Impossible prison* (1980) that most types of French prisons did not conform to the penitentiary ideal realized at La Petite Rocquette.[5]

Italy also failed to realize the disciplinary ideal of the penitentiary, either before or after unification in 1861. Italy's experience with prison reform was, at best, incomplete and frustrating. Italians before and after unification shared in the general European enthusiasm for the penitentiary. Indeed, many Italians, in homage to Cesare Beccaria, felt obligated to participate in the worldwide debate on crime and punishment throughout the nineteenth century. Italian reformers and governments also attempted to realize the penitentiary ideal across the peninsula both before and after unification.

But the disciplinary regime of the penitentiary was not successfully established in Italy, either before unification or during the liberal era. For a variety of reasons, some of them financial, the Italian government failed to establish a unified prison system after unification. Although the Italian Parliament passed the requisite laws and regulations for such a prison system, much of this legislation remained, in contemporaries' words, a "dead letter." Some reforms began in the Giolittian era, but as late as 1904, the Socialist Filippo Turati declared that Italy's prisons were simply "tombs of the living."

In his excellent brief study on Italian prisons, *Carcere e società civile* (1973), Guido Neppi Modona argued that the "immobilism" that characterized Italian prison reform was a deliberate ploy on the part of the ruling class to separate and destroy Italy's criminal population. He also contended that the brutal nature of the Italian prison system actually made it easier to govern and thus inhibited change.

The uneven development of the penitentiary before unification helps explain the halting and incomplete nature of prison reform in Italy after unification, as well. The first chapter of this study concerns prison reform in the preunification Italian states. In this era, two Italian states—the Kingdom of Sardinia-Piedmont and the Grand Duchy of Tuscany—laid the foundations for prison reform in Italy. Both states, however, had different conceptions of the ideal penitentiary. As a consequence, the development of the penitentiary in Italy was by no means unified, a fact that did not bode well for the postunification period. The Kingdom of Sardinia-Piedmont adopted the Auburn system of prison discipline, or work in common during the day and cellular isolation only at night. The Grand Duchy of Tuscany, however, attempted to implement the Philadelphia (or Pennsylvania) system of prison discipline, or continual cellular isolation. The idea of prison reform and of a modern prison system remained a sketchy and incomplete idea in the other Italian states, although prison reformers and intellectuals participated in the debate on the best system of prison discipline. This debate would color the evolution of the prison system after unification.

The second and third chapters deal with prison reform from unification in 1861 to 1887. Throughout this period, Italian prison reformers attempted to fashion a unified prison system for all of Italy. In particular, Martino Beltrani-Scalia, a prison inspector and eventual director general of the prison system, offered a vision of a unified prison system for the entire peninsula. But the proposals that he and others set forth met with no resolution, as the prison question became tied inextricably to the question of a unified penal code. Consequently, the few laws that were passed on prison reform turned out to be paper reforms. Lack of money also plagued reform efforts. This pattern of inaction and inertia afflicted the entire period, and no clear settlement of the prison question had appeared by 1887.

The fourth chapter concerns the emergence of the positive school of criminology. The ideas of Cesare Lombroso and his followers stimulated further discussion and debate on the prison question in Italy, but in a negative way. Lombroso and his disciples called into question the entire purpose of the prison. They advocated treating criminals medically rather than trying to rehabilitate them. These ideas challenged the classical school of criminology and perhaps slowed the development of the penitentiary in Italy.

The fifth chapter deals with the major reform of the period—the Giuseppe Zanardelli penal code of January 1890 and the general regulations of the prison system of 1891. The Zanardelli penal code implemented Beltrani-Scalia's long standing goal of the introduction of the progressive system of prison discipline in Italy. The general regulations, passed in 1891, realized Beltrani-Scalia's vision of a disciplinary regime in the Italian prisons. In particular, Beltrani-Scalia sought to codify and detail the duties of all types of personnel in the prison, as well as the duties, obligations, and goals for the inmates. Every aspect of prison life was laid out in minute detail.

Chapters six and seven gauge the effectiveness of Beltrani-Scalia's reform. For all of the plans and hopes, the prison regulations failed. Calls were made for further reform almost as soon as they were passed. The prisons of Italy, far from fulfilling this disciplinary regime, remained much as they had been in the preunification era. The entire period was marred by a lack of reform, even during the Giolittian liberal era of 1900–1914, the subject of chapter eight. Again, the primary stumbling block remained the lack of money needed to transform the material conditions of the Italian prisons.

Overall, prison reform took place only on a limited scale in Italy during the liberal era. Although the requisite legislation had been passed by 1891, the theory remained just theory. In practice, Italy's prisons rarely lived up to the image of a place of punishment and rehabilitation. The prison personnel, including both the guards and the administrators, also failed to perform their jobs as expected, and the history of the prison system was as much a tale of their continual corruption and competition with each other, as it was a story of unfulfilled promises and paper reforms. The prison system in Italy created a permanent "prison class" not so much because the disciplinary regime was established but because it was never actually realized, except on paper.

This study relies on extensive archival and published materials. Numerous treatises on prison reform, newspapers and journals of the day, and the Italian parliamentary papers help clarify the success or failure of the idea of the penitentiary in Italy before and after unification in 1861. The archive of the director general of the prisons, located in the Archivio Centrale dello Stato in Rome, provides official reports, investigative inquiries, and general information on the day-to-day operations of Italy's prisons. Although archival material is scant for the period before 1885, many of the circulars and investigative reports of the pre–1885 period were published either by the Ministry of the Interior or in the semi-official journals of the prison system, *Effemeride carceraria* and *Rivista di discipline carcerarie.*

Obviously, most of the available sources offer an official and administrative description and analysis of Italy's prisons. Information on the prisoners themselves remains largely incomplete and sketchy, although the reports of visitors to the prisons provide a sense of the life of the inmates. Letters from the inmates to the prison administration also offer some of the prisoners' perceptions of the Italian prison system.

Notes

1.   David Garland, *Punishment and Modern Society: A Study in Social Theory* (Chicago: University of Chicago Press, 1990), 134.

2.   For an excellent critique of Foucault's ideas, see ibid., especially 157–176.

3.   Michael Ignatieff, *A Just Measure of Pain: The Penitentiary in the Industrial Revolution, 1750–1850* (New York: Pantheon, 1978), 214–215.

4.   Gordon Wright, *Between the Guillotine and Liberty: Two Centuries of the Crime Problem in France* (Oxford: Oxford Univ. Press, 1983), especially 22–23.

5.   Michael Ignatieff, "State, Civil Society, and Total Institutions: A Critique of Recent Social Histories of Punishment," in *Social Control and the State*, eds. Stanley Cohen and Andrew Scull (New York: St. Martin's Press, 1983), 75–105.

2

Prison Reform in Preunification Italy

The penitentiary came to Italy before national unification. Like many Europeans, Italian intellectuals and officials were drawn to the idea of the penitentiary by the 1820s. Although all preunification states in Italy searched for the ideal system of prison discipline, only the Kingdom of Sardinia-Piedmont and the Grand Duchy of Tuscany actually attempted to realize grand schemes of prison reform. But these two states chose different methods of prison discipline, and the other Italian states realized only minimal improvement in their prison systems during this period. Thus, the prison's development before unification was as uneven as the economic and social systems in the various preunification states.

Regardless of the different approaches to prison discipline that eventually emerged, all Italians began their study of crime and punishment with the work of Cesare Beccaria. Although Beccaria did not "invent" the penitentiary, his criticisms of the criminal justice system of the Old Regime certainly paved the way for the revolution in penal practices that began in the late-eighteenth century. Indeed, later Italian penal reformers unhesitatingly acknowledged their intellectual debt to this great reformer, as did other Europeans.[1]

Beccaria was born in 1738 to modestly wealthy parents. After earning a law degree in 1758, the young nobleman actively participated in the intellectual life of his home, Milan. He visited several of the fashionable literary clubs and eventually joined the *Accademia dei pugni* (Academy of Fisticuffs). This small band of intellectuals met regularly to discuss their own writings and those of the leading French *philosophes*.[2]

On the suggestion of the group's leader, Pietro Verri, Beccaria initiated a study of the prevailing system of European criminal law. In the course of his research, he discovered that the existing laws lacked clarity and were frequently contradictory. Judges enjoyed excessive latitude in their interpretation of the laws. Torture was commonly used to extract confessions from the accused. Most minor crimes were punished with flogging or physical dismemberment, such as cutting off the hand of a thief. Throughout Europe, the death penalty, often preceded by physical torture, was the accepted punishment for a vast array of crimes.[3]

Beccaria offered a prescription for these ills in his brief essay, *Dei delitti e delle pene* (*An Essay on Crimes and Punishments*), first published in 1764. He argued that written laws, easily comprehensible to all members of society, must serve as the basis for all punishments. Judges must inflict only the punishments required by law. Punishment should prevent the criminal from repeating his crime and deter the rest of society from committing a similar infraction. Punishments should thus be designed to convince both the criminal and free citizens that the pain of punishment outweighed the pleasure of crime.[4]

Beccaria further argued that punishment should not be brutal. In his opinion, neither torture nor the death penalty served a useful purpose, as neither penalty would effectively stop future crime. The sight of the criminal's death would make but a "fleeting" impression on the observer's mind. Beccaria's notion of the ideal punishment was a type of perpetual slavery in which the condemned, in chains, publicly performed hard labor. Such a punishment would inspire the individual citizen with so much fear of similarly losing his freedom that he would avoid a life of crime.[5]

These ideas on crime and punishment were by no means unique to Beccaria. Others in the Italian peninsula, such as the scholar Ludovico Antonio Muratori (1672–1750), had criticized the obscurity and irrationality of the eighteenth-century legal system.[6] The French *philosophe* and political theorist, Baron de Montesquieu (1689–1755), also had written that a good legislator should prevent crimes rather than just punish criminals. He had also stressed the need for the punishment to fit the crime and called for the abolition of judicial torture.[7]

Beccaria's treatise won widespread renown precisely because it synthesized, in an elegant and brief essay, the prevailing criticisms of the criminal justice system of the Old Regime. By 1767, the book had been translated into numerous foreign languages, including French, Polish, English, and German. Almost all the French *philosophes*, especially Voltaire, praised Beccaria's call for the codification of laws and the abolition of torture. Not all could agree, however, on the need to eliminate the death penalty.[8]

The Church severely criticized Beccaria's work and placed it on the Index. A Venetian monk, Ferdinando Facchinei, immediately penned a lengthy critique after the book's publication. He portrayed Beccaria as a sacrilegious individualist who failed to understand the deterrent effect of the death penalty. The life of hard labor that Beccaria proposed in lieu of the death penalty resembled too closely the current working conditions of the poor and thus could not keep them from crime.[9]

But this criticism did not stop the influence of the treatise. Most significantly, Beccaria's essay contributed directly to the reform in penal legislation that began in the 1780s. The best known example of concrete change occurred, in fact, in the Italian peninsula. In 1786, Grand Duke Pietro Leopoldo of the Grand Duchy of

Tuscany promulgated a new law code based entirely on principles laid down in *Dei delitti e delle pene*. The code ended the use of torture and abolished the death penalty. It provided for various public punishments, ranging from flogging to hard labor in chains. As Beccaria had prescribed, those condemned to hard labor would work in public and wear a card that named their offense and the length of their sentence, in the expectation that this would instill fear in the onlooking public.[10]

Beccaria never abandoned his belief that punishment must be public in order to deter crime. In the early 1790s, he also began to advocate the use of the prison for minor crimes. He stated that these prisons should have a degree of discipline and that the accused should always be separated from the convicted. But the prison should be clearly visible to the citizens of the local community to remind them that crime would not go unpunished.[11]

Beccaria's interest in the prison paralleled a growing belief among Europeans that the prison could be used for both punishment and the correction of criminals. Traditionally, the prison had been used as a holding pen for the accused who were awaiting trial. By the late eighteenth century, the Englishman John Howard (1726–1791) had developed the idea that a cellular prison, in which silence and labor were emphasized, would transform the criminal into a useful member of society.[12] At the same time, Howard's friend, Jeremy Bentham (1748–1842), developed his plan for a penitentiary regime, the Panopticon.[13] In France, the new revolutionary government ordered the construction of a national network of prisons in which the implicit goal would be the rehabilitation of the offender.[14]

As the penitentiary gained widespread acceptance, prison reformers attempted to organize the prison so that it would most effectively achieve the twin, if seemingly contradictory, goals of punishment and rehabilitation. In the 1820s, American prison reformers designed two different models of prison discipline. The first of these, known as the Auburn or congregate system, permitted the inmates to work together during the day, but in complete silence. Cellular isolation would occur only at night. The other system, called the Philadelphia or separate system, called for continual cellular isolation. Each prisoner would work and eat in his own cell, under the rule of silence, and would have no contact whatsoever with other inmates.[15]

These rival systems captured the attention of European prison reformers. Several countries, including France, Britain, and Prussia, dispatched representatives to compare the two approaches. Although the two systems were actually quite similar—both stressed silence and labor as key elements in a rehabilitative program—European prison reformers exhausted their writing skills debating the merits of the two approaches during the 1830s and 1840s.[16]

Advocates of prison reform in the preunification states of Italy actively participated in this highly charged debate. Men such as Count Carlo Iliarone Petitti di Roreto of the Kingdom of Sardinia-Piedmont and Carlo Cattaneo of the Kingdom of Lombardy-Venetia voiced their support for one or the other system in various liberal journals and at the meetings of the Congress of Italian Scientists. Like many Europeans, they advocated prison reform for humanitarian reasons. But more importantly, they promoted such reform as part of a larger liberal program of social, economic, and political renovation. The realization of this liberal agenda, which included prison reform, the development of a railway network, free trade, and a free press, was considered crucial if the Italian states hoped to industrialize and compete with Britain and France.[17]

Count Carlo Iliarone Petitti di Roreto (1790–1850) earned renown throughout Italy as a champion of liberal reform. The son of a poor but noble family, Petitti studied law at the University of Genoa and eventually became an advisor to the government of Sardinia-Piedmont. He frequently submitted articles to the liberal journal, *Annali universali di statistica*, on such topics as poor relief and child labor laws. He also wrote several important works on the need for a railroad system. And he actively promoted prison reform in his native Sardinia-Piedmont.[18]

Petitti first revealed an interest in prison reform after a visit to a Piedmontese prison in 1835. He found, to his dismay, that prisoners lived in common, were undisciplined, and easily purchased wine and other spirits in the prison canteen. Further inspection of the other prisons of Sardinia-Piedmont stimulated his decision to develop a comprehensive program of prison reform for Piedmont.[19]

As evidenced by his major work on prison reform, *Della condizione attuale delle carceri e dei mezzi di migliorarla (The Current State of the Prisons and the Ways of Improving Them)* (1840), Petitti clearly believed in the reformative possibilities of the prison. Influenced by the work of the French prison reformer, Charles Lucas[20], he criticized the Philadelphia system. Extended cellular isolation would not lead to the rehabilitation of the inmates. At best, cellular isolation could be used effectively on a short-term basis for the accused and for prisoners sentenced to less than two years. Like many reformers, he thought that extended cellular isolation would harm the health of the inmates. He also shared the common belief that Mediterranean peoples, with their presumed expansive personalities, stood in particular need of some sort of social contact. Finally, this pragmatic government official argued that the Philadelphia system would be costly to implement, and that it could never completely eliminate communication between prisoners.[21]

Petitti thus favored the Auburn system of prison discipline, at least for long-term prisoners. He stressed that it would be less expensive because it would be easier to adapt existing buildings to the congregate system, particularly in Italy where so many of the prisons were housed in old fortresses and former convents. He also argued that the prisoner would be less likely to suffer mental illness if he had some contact with other people. Most importantly, Petitti argued, the prisoner would learn a useful trade in a semi-industrial setting. The penitentiary would thus pay for itself and the prisoner would be prepared to support himself by honest means after his sentence ended.[22]

Petitti did not limit himself to the debate on the merits of the Philadelphia and Auburn systems of prison management. He also offered a comprehensive scheme for the reorganization of the prisons in Sardinia-Piedmont. He envisioned a centralized, rationally organized system, modeled after that of France and Great Britain. A director general of the prisons, dependent on the Ministry of the Interior, would oversee the entire system. Separate prisons would be established for the accused, for female and juvenile offenders, and for short- and long-term prisoners.[23]

Petitti called for two types of prisons for the convicted criminal. The first of these, the *carceri repressive,* would house those prisoners sentenced to less than two years. Petitti did not believe these prisoners would be in prison long enough to undergo a reformatory program. Consequently, he encouraged a harsh disciplinary regime in which fear of return replaced rehabilitation. This severe regime would also deter honest folk from committing crime. True to his belief that cellular isolation was an excellent way to frighten prisoners into submission, Petitti recommended the use of cellular isolation, with the rule of silence, during the entire sentence. Inmates would receive religious and moral education on a regular basis and would be obliged to work.[24]

The second type of prison, the *carceri correttive,* would be reserved for long-term prisoners. As the name implies, Petitti thought that the regime in these prisons could correct the delinquent. Organized according to the Auburn system, all inmates would be subjected to the same disciplinary regime. The prisoner's day would be regimented and disciplined to teach the inmate obedience and the value of hard work. Prisoners would be taught a trade and given regular moral and religious instruction. They would wear a uniform, march in step, and maintain the rule of silence. Violation of any rule would be severely punished.[25]

Petitti did not think that all prisoners would respond equally to the reformatory program of the *carceri correttive.* The inmates who resisted the discipline of the penitentiary would have to be "coerced" into obedience, though not in a brutal fashion. He further warned that the guards would have to keep a sharp eye out for the "hypocrisy" of those wily prisoners who would feign acceptance of the reformative program in order to win special favors and leniency. Regardless of the result of the program, Petitti did believe that the inmate would leave the prison "if . . . not yet virtuous . . . at least reasonable" and likely to calculate against future criminal acts.[26]

Petitti's ideas on prison discipline attracted the interest and attention of advocates of prison reform throughout Italy. In 1843, Petitti presented his ideas for a mixed system of prison discipline to the Congress of Italian Scientists held in

Lucca. These annual meetings, initiated in 1839, attracted moderate liberals from Italy and Europe and provided a forum for the discussion of such issues as prison reform, the construction of railroads, and the rationalization of agriculture. Although Petitti made a valiant effort to convince the delegates of the efficacy of his proposed system, the majority of them expressed overwhelming support for the Philadelphia system as "completely preferable in its moral, hygienic, penal, and economic aspects."[27]

The delegates at the Congress had undoubtedly been influenced by the work of the prominent Lombard intellectual, Carlo Cattaneo (1801–1869). A student of the legal theorist Gian Domenico Romagnosi (1761–1833), Cattaneo established a reputation as a liberal reformer in the 1830s. He used the pages of Milan's liberal journal, *Annali universali di statistica*, as well as those of his own journal, *Il Politecnico*, to promote agricultural, industrial, and political reform.[28]

The breadth of Cattaneo's knowledge won him the respect of the Austrian government, and he was frequently asked to prepare reports on various subjects, including prison reform. After he had completed a study of the penal practices of the United States and Great Britain, he wrote several articles on the subject for *Il Politecnico*.[29]

In "Delle carceri" ("On Prisons") (1840), the lengthiest of these articles, Cattaneo argued that a properly organized prison system could both rehabilitate the criminal and also deter future crime. The communal prisons of the past had not accomplished these goals; rather, the free association between the hardened criminal and the youthful offender simply created and perpetuated a criminal class. A convinced environmentalist, Cattaneo pointed out that the Auburn system could not prevent some degree of communication, and therefore corruption, between prisoners.[30]

Cattaneo asserted that only the Philadelphia system could fulfill the twin goals of rehabilitation and deterrence. Cellular isolation created the ideal environment for the rehabilitation of the offender because it eliminated any possibility of further corruption. Alone in his silent cell, the criminal would gradually see the error of his ways. Cattaneo described the normal course of such a transformation:

> Left to himself in his solitary cell, he will first abandon himself to rage, thoughts of revenge, and curses of anger. But weariness will follow this violence; the silence which greets his vain cries will gradually make him understand the futility of resistance; and he will gradually realize his impotence in the face of the law.[31]

Cattaneo cited statistics from the American prisons to refute the commonly held belief that constant cellular isolation drove man to madness. He also dismissed the idea that the regime was too soft simply because it provided the prisoner with adequate food and a warm bed. He argued instead that all criminals would prefer the undisciplined communal prison of the past to the austere and demanding cellular prison. Indeed, he maintained that the harsh regime would deter many who might otherwise take up a life of crime. To skeptics who persisted in their criticisms of the Philadelphia system, Cattaneo asserted that if nothing else, cellular isolation made criminals no worse than they had been before incarceration.[32]

Moderate liberals like Petitti and Cattaneo clearly viewed prison reform as a necessary part of any liberal program for change, renovation, and improvement of Italian society. But the actual programs for prison reform varied from state to state in the peninsula. Only two states, the Kingdom of Sardinia-Piedmont and the Grand Duchy of Tuscany devised comprehensive programs for prison reform before unification, with Piedmont adopting the Auburn system and Tuscany embracing the Philadelphia system. The other Italian states, most notably the Kingdom of the Two Sicilies, lagged far behind Sardinia-Piedmont and Tuscany in prison reform and adopted changes in a piecemeal fashion. Even in the more advanced states, the plans for prison reform were realized slowly and partially.

As in the case of so many other improvements and changes in Italian society before unification, the Kingdom of Sardinia-Piedmont led the way in prison reform, initiating extensive improvements in the material conditions of its prisons during the Restoration era. In the 1830s, King Carlo Alberto (1831–1848) launched a series of reforms that won him the admiration of Petitti and other Piedmontese liberals. He first abolished torture and then promulgated a new law code (1839) that declared rehabilitation of the prisoner the end and purpose of punishment. After consultation with Petitti, the king ordered the construction of three new penitentiaries, all to be organized according to the Auburn system of prison discipline. Work was also begun on special prisons for women and for juveniles. Finally, he provided that the inmates of the custodial prisons (*carceri giudiziarie*) would be separated according to religion, age, and alleged crime.[33]

By the 1850s, two of the three penitentiaries were completed and in operation at Alessandria and Oneglia. The Auburn-style prisons were subjected to a disciplinary regime based on Petitti's ideas. All prisoners were obliged to work, in complete silence. Inmates who refused to work received smaller rations and were subjected to severe discipline. Violations of prison regulations resulted in a maximum punishment of solitary confinement, in chains, with only bread and water to eat.[34]

The new penitentiaries thus fulfilled the first aspect of Petitti's plans for a comprehensive reform of the Piedmontese prison system. The actual operation of the penitentiaries left much to be desired. The key problem proved to be the poor design and unhealthy locale of both prisons. The cells at Alessandria, for example, were built without windows. The abnormally high mortality rate at Alessandria led a government investigator to conclude that the small cells, the unhealthy site, and the rule of silence all worked together to kill inmates at an excessively fast pace.[35]

The suggested reorganization of the custodial prisons also proved difficult to achieve. The Council of Prisons, empowered to make annual visits to the prisons of the realm, consistently lamented the lack of discipline in the custodial prisons. It also urged the construction of new prisons to replace the old, ramshackle buildings. In response to the latter demand, the minister of the interior, Urbano Rattazzi (1808–1873), sponsored legislation in 1857 that called for the construction of new cellular custodial prisons in all major cities. The first projects, begun in 1857 in Turin and Genoa, were slowed, however, by a chronic shortage of money.[36]

Like the Kingdom of Sardinia-Piedmont, the Grand Duchy of Tuscany initiated prison reform in the 1830s. Until then, the Tuscan prisons, especially the custodial ones (*carceri pretoriali*), were largely unregulated and disorganized. Prisoners communicated freely between themselves and with people on the outside. Hard labor, in chains, in the *bagni penali* of Livorno, Pisa, and Portoferraio, was the primary punishment for major crimes like homicide.[37]

Carlo Peri, who was eventually appointed the director general of the Tuscan prison system, led the penal reform movement. Under his guidance, the first set of general prison regulations separated the accused from the convicted. Cellular segregation was ordered to be used whenever possible, and prisoners were subjected to the rule of silence. The regulations also ordered that the windows in the custodial prisons be modified so as to prevent communication with the outside world.[38]

The regulations established the Penal and Corrective Prison (*Carceri delle Murate*) in Florence as the key reformatory institution for long-term offenders. Prisoners were segregated from each other "at night, during religious services, during meals, and during walks," but they were permitted to work together in small groups. Recidivists, however, were confined to their cells at all times. Of course, prisoners were forbidden to speak unless they had received permission from a guard.[39]

With the support and encouragement of Peri, a new penal code in 1853 eliminated all contact between inmates and introduced the Philadelphia system for all Tuscan prisons. But in 1859, Dr. Carlo Morelli reported that the use of extended cellular isolation in the penitentiary of Volterra harmed the health of the prisoners. In the wake of his findings, the Tuscan government decided to alter but not eliminate the use of the Philadelphia system. Prisoners would be subjected to cellular isolation for a maximum of ten years, after which they would be permitted to work in common with other inmates. Well-behaved inmates would be given the option of completing their sentences in an agricultural penal colony, established on the island of Pianosa in 1858. Even though Peri opposed these revisions of the Philadelphia system, they were accepted and implemented on the eve of national unification.[40]

Like many prison reformers, Peri absolutely opposed the use of Tuscany's three *bagni penali* at Livorno, Portoferraio, and Pisa. Unlike Beccaria a century earlier, he could see no benefits coming from hard labor in public. Indeed, he argued that continual exposure to the outside world would further corrupt the already hardened criminal. He thus applauded the government's decision in the 1840s to stop using the *forzati* to clean public streets, and he wholeheartedly supported the decision to close the *bagni* in 1850.[41]

The Austrian-dominated Kingdom of Lombardy-Venetia lagged far behind Piedmont and Tuscany in prison reform. Although it was the most economically advanced state in the peninsula during the restoration era, it implemented few of Cattaneo's suggestions for the improvement of the prison system. The Austrian Code of 1803, which remained in effect until 1852, provided for the sentences of *carcere duro* and *carcere durissimo*. This latter punishment involved chaining prisoners to walls and then feeding them a minimal diet of bread, water, and occasional meat.[42]

The famous political prisoner Silvio Pellico (1789–1854) also described a prison system reminiscent of the pre-Enlightenment age. Prior to his transfer to the Spielberg in Bohemia, Pellico was imprisoned in Milan and Venice. In Milan's prison of Santa Margherita, a converted convent like many Italian prisons, Pellico was not subjected to any sort of disciplinary regime. Indeed, the guards, who earned extra money selling wine to the prisoners, were disconcerted to discover that Pellico was a teetotaler. He described his cell as "dark and foul, its windows with panes not of glass but of paper, its walls soiled by coarse and clumsy drawings."[43]

Lombardy did, however have one penal institution that earned the praise of all who visited it, the Casa di Correzione in Milan. Completed in 1764, the prison was well-ventilated and had clean and spacious cells. "Jail fever," the typhus that often swept through prisons, was uncommon because the prison was regularly cleaned. The inmates enjoyed a healthy diet and also gained work experience in textiles.[44]

Like the Kingdom of Lombardy-Venetia, the Papal States failed to adopt a systematic program for prison reform. Torture was still used in some prisons as late as the 1830s.[45] Only the prisons of Rome experienced a degree of reform. By the 1840s, inmates were segregated according to age, sex, and crime. The prisons were also inspected on a regular basis.[46]

The Papal States also had one noteworthy institution for juveniles, San Michele. Founded in 1703, this institution stressed discipline and labor in a reformative program, just as later reformers would. During his visit in the late eighteenth century, Howard praised the prison and expressed particular fondness for an inscription on the wall that stated "It is of little advantage to restrain the bad by punishment unless you render them good by discipline."[47]   The success of this institution prompted a student of the prisons of Rome, Carlo-Luigi Morichini, to argue that the papacy invented the modern penitentiary.[48]

The improved conditions of the prisons of Piedmont and Tuscany were not mirrored in the prisons of the Kingdom of the Two Sicilies. Granted, there was a veneer of reform. New prison regulations were passed as early as 1817. Provisions were later made for annual inspections of all prisons. Two new penitentiaries, one in Avellino and the other in Palermo, were built in the 1820s and 1830s. Several Neapolitans, most notably Pasquale Stanislao Mancini (1817–1888) and Ferdinando Volpicella (1803–1888), contributed to the ongoing debate on the merits of the Auburn and Philadelphia systems.[49]

The actual state of the prisons belied the extent of prison reform. Luigi Settembrini (1813–1876) spent time as a political prisoner in several Neapolitan prisons. He later offered a nauseating account of his stay in the custodial prison of La Vicaria during 1849:

> In the prison of the nobles, about 400 men were tormented by the stench, the darkness, the insects; never comforted with clean air accused and the convicted mixed together, the political prisoners mixed with the murderers. . . . When the windows are closed at night, one can see and touch a heavy air, a dense smoke formed by tobacco mixed with miasma. . . . From the lower prison, a stench arises . . . a stench of rotting human flesh, a stench which can have no other name than the stench of La Vicaria.[50]

After his death sentence was commuted to life imprisonment, Settembrini was sent to the *ergastolo* of Santo Stefano. Located on a small island just off the Italian coast, conditions in this prison for long-term criminals were no better than those in La Vicaria. The cells, for example, were designed for four men but often held up to ten. The walls were "black and smoky like the kitchens of peasants." As at La Vicaria, Settembrini found the stench and the heat unbearable.[51]

The English Liberal William E. Gladstone (1809–1898) also offered a vivid and critical account of the prisons of Naples. During a brief visit to southern Italy with his family, Gladstone witnessed the prosecution of political prisoners in the aftermath of the revolutions of 1848. He also visited several prisons to meet some of the men on trial. What he saw of the Neapolitan criminal justice and penal system so horrified him that he decided to publicize his findings by means of two letters to then English prime minister, Lord Aberdeen.[52]

Gladstone painted a grim picture of both La Vicaria and the *bagno* of Nisida.

Echoing Settembrini, he characterized the former prison as a "charnel house" completely devoid of any disciplinary regime. The prison was filthy, overcrowded, and the prisoners mixed freely, regardless of age, sex, or offense. Guards exerted no authority; the "gammoristi" (*camorra*) really controlled the prison.[53]

Gladstone described the *bagno* of Nisida with the same searing detail. The *bagno* was overcrowded, with seventeen men sharing one room. Prisoners were chained together in pairs, and the heavy chains were never removed. Indeed, Gladstone noted that the health of the inmates had visibly deteriorated as a consequence of the harsh regime.[54]

Regardless of his motives, Gladstone's letters on the prisons of Naples galvanized European sensibilities. The letters were rapidly translated into several languages after their initial publication in 1851. British diplomats disseminated the letters across Europe.[55] The legal system of the Kingdom of the Two Sicilies became the object of European derision and distaste. And the prisons of Naples, as Gladstone had described them, became "another name for the extreme of filth and horror."[56]

In the wake of Gladstone's criticisms, the government of the Kingdom of the Two Sicilies made a half-hearted attempt to improve the material conditions of its prisons. Its efforts proved futile, as the money needed to implement a substantial program of prison reform remained elusive. On the eve of national unification, the prison system of southern Italy thus compared very unfavorably to that of Sardinia-Piedmont and Tuscany.[57]

What then can we conclude about prison reform in preunification Italy? Clearly, the Italian states in those years had no shortage of enthusiastic advocates of prison reform. Like many Europeans, these reformers saw the institution of the penitentiary as the ideal solution to crime. But the successful implementation of their proposals varied from state to state. Piedmont and Tuscany far outpaced the rest of the peninsula, but their very success would prove an obstacle after unification, as each claimed precedence in prison reform. Thus, the uneven development of the prison systems in the preunification states, combined with a shortage of money, was to hinder the creation of a national prison system after 1861.

It should also be noted that this disparate development was by no means restricted to Italy's preunification prison systems. The economic and social systems of the various Italian states also manifested uneven growth, with Piedmont and Tuscany being more economically advanced than the Kingdom of the Two Sicilies. The very different nature of the preunification states impeded the successful creation of a nation-state after 1861.

Notes

1. The English utilitarian philosopher and penal reformer, Jeremy Bentham, proclaimed in reference to Beccaria: "O my master, first evangelist of Reason, you who have raised Italy so far above England, and I would add above France, were it not that Helevetius . . . had already assisted you." See Elie Halévy, *The Growth of Philosophic Radicalism*, trans. Mary Morris (New York: Macmillan, 1928), 21.

2. Marcello Maestro, *Cesare Beccaria and the Origins of Penal Reform* (Philadelphia: Temple Univ. Press, 1973), 4–10.

3. On Verri's influence, see ibid., 10–12; and Franco Venturi, *Settecento riformatore* (Turin: Einaudi, 1969), 671–733. On the eighteenth-century penal practices, consult Isser Woloch, *Eighteenth-Century Europe* (New York: W. W. Norton, 1982), 163–174; and Maestro, *Cesare Beccaria*, 12–19.

4. Cesare Beccaria, *Dei delitti e delle pene*, ed. Franco Venturi (Turin: Einaudi, 1965), 9–104. This edition also includes an extensive selection of documents relating to the European reaction to Beccaria's treatise.

5. Ibid., especially 38–44 and 59–70.

6. Maestro, *Cesare Beccaria*, 17.

7. Baron de Montesquieu, *The Spirit of the Laws*, trans. Thomas Nugent (New York: Hafner, 1949), I: 81–92.

8. See a selection of the various responses in Beccaria, *Dei delitti*, 425–650.

9. Maestro, *Cesare Beccaria*, 37. Excerpts from Facchinei's critique, *Note ed osservazioni sul libro intitolato Dei delitti e delle pene*, are printed in Beccaria, 164–177.

10. The complete text of the Code is printed in Beccaria, *Dei delitti*, 258–300.

11. Cesare Beccaria, *Opere*, ed. Sergio Romagnoli (Florence: Sansoni, 1958), II: 705–741.

12. On Howard and the origins of the penitentiary in England, see Ignatieff, *A Just Measure of Pain*, especially 44–79.

13. Halévy, *The Growth*, 82–85; and Leslie Stephen, *The English Utilitarians* (New York: Peter Smith, 1950), I: 194–205.

14. Gordon Wright, *Between the Guillotine and Liberty* (New York: Oxford Univ. Press, 1983), 25–33.

15. David Rothman, *The Discovery of the Asylum* (Boston: Little, Brown, and Company, 1971), 79–105. The two types of prison discipline were named for the cities in which they first emerged—Auburn, New York, and Philadelphia, Pennsylvania.

16. France, for example, sent Gustave Beaumont and Alexis de Tocqueville. They both voiced support for the Philadelphia system. See Wright, *Between the Guillotine*, 63–66.

17. Stuart Woolf, *A History of Italy, 1700–1860: The Social Constraints of Political Change* (London: Methuen and Co., 1979), 316–360; and Kent Roberts Greenfield, *Economics and Liberalism in the Risorgimento*, 2nd ed. (Baltimore;

Johns Hopkins Univ. Press, 1965), 147–149.

18.	On Petitti's career, see the biographical sketch by Gian Mario Bravo in Carlo Iliarone Petitti di Roreto, *Opere scelte*, ed. Gian Mario Bravo (Turin: Einaudi, 1969), II: 1000-1011.

19..	Anna Capelli, *La buona compagnia: Utopia e realtà carceraria nell'Italia del Risorgimento* (Milan: Franco Angeli, 1988), 144–145.

20.	Charles Lucas emerged as an advocate of prison reform in the 1820s. He vociferously criticized the Philadelphia system, considering it dangerous to the health and rehabilitation of inmates. See, for example, Charles Lucas, *Du système pénal et du système répressif en général, de la peine de mort en particulier* (Paris: Bechet, 1827).

21.	Petitti, *Opere scelte*, I: 460–471. It should be noted that Petitti offered typical criticisms of the Philadelphia system. See Rothman, *The Discovery*, 86–88, for example.

22.	Ibid., I: 457–460.

23.	Ibid., I: 501–512.

24.	Ibid., I: 524–526.

25.	Ibid., I: 527–543.

26.	Ibid., I: 492, 527.

27.	Ibid., I: 852–855. On the congresses, consult Greenfield, *Economics*, 278–281.

28.	On the liberal politics of the *Annali* and *il Politecnico*, see Greenfield, *Economics*, 150–190. On Cattaneo's intellectual development, see Clara Lovett, *Carlo Cattaneo and the Politics of the Risorgimento* (The Hague: Martinus Nijhoff, 1972), 2–36.

29.	Lovett, *Carlo Cattaneo*, 22–23.

30.	Carlo Cattaneo, *Scritti politici*, ed. Mario Boneschi (Florence: LeMonnier, 1964), I: 285–327.

31.	Ibid., 302.

32.	Ibid., especially 305–307.

33.	Martino Beltrani-Scalia, *Sul governo e sulla riforma delle carceri in Italia. Saggio storico e teorico* (Turin: Favale, 1867), 420–423; Dario Melossi and Massimo Pavarini, *The Prison and the Factory*, trans. Glynis Cousin (New Jersey: Barnes and Noble, 1981), 85–86; and Enrico Pessina, *Il diritto penale in Italia da Cesare Beccaria sino alla promulgazione del codice penale vigente (1764–1890)*, in *Enciclopedia del diritto penale italiano*, ed. Luigi Lucchini (Milan: n.p., 1906), II: 600.

34.	Capelli, *La buona compangia*, 269–271.

35.	Ibid., 270–272.

36.	Beltrani-Scalia, *Sul governo e sulla riforma*, 429–435. The custodial prison in Turin, for example, was not completed until 1869.

37.	Carlo Peri, *Cenni sulla riforma del sistema penitenziario in Toscana* (Florence: Penitenziario di Firenze, 1848), 4–14.

38. Ibid., 15–41; Beltrani-Scalia, *Sul governo e sulla riforma*, 440–445.

39. Peri, *Cenni sulla riforma*, 41–73, 119–125.

40. Capelli, *La buona compagnia*, 322–325; Beltrani-Scalia, *Sul governo e sulla riforma*, 445–450.

41. Peri, *Cenni sulla riforma*, 87–92; Capelli, *La buona compagnia*, 313.

42. Melossi and Pavarini, *The Prison*, 86; and John A. Davis, *Conflict and Control: Law and Order in Nineteenth-Century Italy* (Atlantic Highlands, N.J.: Humanities Press Intl., 1988), 154.

43. Silvio Pellico, *My Prisons*, trans. I. G. Capaldi, S.J. (London: Oxford Univ. Press, 1963), 1–7, 16.

44. See John Howard's enthusiastic description in his *The State of the Prisons* (New York: E. P. Dutton and Co., 1929), 98–100. The Lombard economist Giuseppe Pecchio updated Howard's account in 1819 for the liberal journal, *Il Conciliatore*. See his descriptive article, "Casa di correzione di Milano," in *Il Conciliatore*, ed. Vittore Branca (Florence: Le Monnier, 1948), I: 496–503.

45. Beltrani-Scalia, *Sul governo e sulla riforma*, 446.

46. Carlo-Luigi Morichini, *Degli istituti di carità per la sussistenza e l'educazione dei poveri e dei prigionieri in Roma,* 9th ed. (Rome: Stab. Tip. Camerale, 1870), 685–686.

47. Howard, *The State*, 95.

48. Morichini, *Degli istituti*, 790–791. Morichini was eventually named a cardinal.

49. Beltrani-Scalia, *Sul governo e sulla riforma*, 472–473. Volpicella, for example, authored a lengthy treatise on prison reform, *Delle prigioni e del loro migliore ordinamento* in 1837. Begun on the recommendation of the Ministry of the Interior of the Kingdom of the Two Sicilies, Volpicella explored the history of the prison and then offered a theoretical discussion of the best type of prison and of the purpose of punishment. An advocate of the Auburn system of prison discipline, Volpicella recommended that the prison be a place of punishment and of rehabilitation. Like the other reformers of his day, his program also stressed the importance of education (religious and civil) and labor in prison. To prevent corruption, he argued that the rule of silence should be strictly enforced in any prison system. The prison guards must serve as role models for the inmates, inspiring them to an honest life by example. And the prison director must be a father figure, guiding the inmates back onto the path of virtue with a firm but kind hand. For further information, see Ferdinando Volpicella, *Delle prigioni e del loro migliore ordinamento* (Naples: Fibreno, 1837), especially 87–219; and Petitti, I: 420.

50. Luigi Settembrini, *Ricordanze della mia vita e Scritti autobiografici*, ed. Mario Themelly (Milan: Feltrinelli, 1961), 144–145.

51. Ibid., 316–317.

52. Richard Shannon, *Gladstone* (London: Hamish Hamilton, 1982), 232.

53.   William E. Gladstone, *A Letter to the Earl of Aberdeen on the State Prosecutions of the Neapolitan Government* (London: John Murray, 1851), 15–16. The *camorra*, an organized criminal association, first emerged in the prisons of Naples during the 1830s.

Gladstone's description of La Vicaria was seconded in 1851 by another member of the English Parliament, Alexander Baillie-Cochrane. The lower level of the prison particularly disgusted him:

> The moment the last gate was unbarred we found ourselves in a place which it would require the imagination of Dante to paint. . . . Some were lying on the floor; others crowded together on the miserable truckle beds, howling and blaspheming. . . . Some had climbed up to the open bars and were jeering at the people on the street. It was vice in all its degradation and horror; human life in a living tomb assisting at the spectacle of its own decay, its own rotteness.

For more on his description of the prisons of Naples, see Major Arthur Griffiths, *Italian Prisons: St. Angelo—The Piombi—The Vicaria—Prisons of the Roman Inquisition* (London: The Grolier Society, n.d.), especially 251–255.

54.   Ibid., 16–17.

55.   Shannon, *Gladstone*, 245. The accuracy of Gladstone's descriptions, as well as his motives, have been explored by several historians of his early career. See Shannon, *Gladstone*, 228–242, and H. C. G. Matthew, *Gladstone, 1809–1874* (Oxford: Clarendon Press, 1986), especially 80–81.

56.   Gladstone, *A Letter*, 15.

57.   Beltrani-Scalia, *Sul governo e sulla riforma,* 472–473.

3

An Uncertain Beginning: Prison Reform in the 1860s

The sad state of the prison systems of preunification Italy did not disappear with the proclamation of the Kingdom of Italy in March 1861. A vast array of legal and financial obstacles slowed the creation of a national prison system. To compound these problems, some members of Parliament and some officials in the prison administration disagreed with the decision to extend the Piedmontese prison system across the Italian peninsula. Persistent financial problems further limited any lasting reforms in the prison system of Italy during the 1860s. But for all of these difficulties, the decade did see the emergence of Martino Beltrani-Scalia, the man who would become the driving force behind prison reform over the next twenty years.

Fashioning a single prison system from the various preunification systems was but one of a host of legislative and administrative problems that confronted the new state. As is well known, the Italian government attempted, with varying degrees of success, to "Piedmontize" the preunification states in order to create a unified country as quickly as possible. King Victor Emmanuel II of Sardinia-Piedmont became the first king of Italy. Sardinia-Piedmont's constitutional Statuto of 1848 became the constitution of the new country. And much to the distress of federalists like Carlo Cattaneo, the administrative structure of the new government was an expansion of the highly centralized Piedmontese model.[1]

It is not surprising, therefore, that the new government chose to adopt the Piedmontese prison system as the model for a national prison system. As in the former Kingdom of Sardinia-Piedmont, all prisons, with the exception of the *bagni penali*,[2] were placed under the administration of the Ministry of the Interior. The director general of the prisons, an office established in 1861, was patterned after that of the inspector general of the prisons of the Kingdom of Sardinia-Piedmont. Although the director general was subordinate to the minister of the interior, he supervised the national prison administration and all of its employees. As was to be expected, the first director general, Giuseppe Boschi, was a Piedmontese lawyer who had worked in the Piedmontese prison administration since the 1850s.[3]

Another important personnel division in the nascent prison administration, also based upon a Piedmontese precedent, was the office of the Inspectorate of Prisons.[4] Four national inspectors, directly subordinate to the director general, were chosen on a yearly basis from among the more prominent officials in the prison administration. Although Piedmontese prison officials dominated the Inspectorate, several of the early officials were selected from among the leading prison officials of the preunification states in an effort to integrate these men into the national prison system.[5] The four inspectors were entrusted with the direct surveillance of the juvenile prisons (*case di custodia*), the custodial prisons (*carceri giudiziarie*), and the penitentiaries (*case di pena*). They were required to make annual reports on the state of these prisons and to assist the director general in the compilation of statistics on the prison population.[6]

Simultaneously with the organization of the prison administration on the Piedmontese model, the Piedmontese prison regulations were extended across Italy. These regulations detailed the personnel, the disciplinary regime, and the standards of food, clothing, and hygiene for each type of prison. The regulations for the custodial prisons, for example, specified that these institutions would house those awaiting trial and those convicted and sentenced to less than one year. Cellular segregation was ordered for all prisoners. Inmates were subjected to the rule of silence and were not allowed to engage in any activity deemed immoral by the prison staff. All prisoners were ordered to work while in prison, unless they were awaiting trial and had the means to support themselves.[7]

But the Kingdom of Sardinia-Piedmont lacked a single comprehensive set of rules that applied to the five types of prisons.[8] Consequently, disciplinary norms differed in the custodial prisons and the penitentiaries. In the former, for example, the prison officials were authorized to use straitjackets and to strap down violent prisoners. Officials in the penitentiaries could only resort to the use of chains in similar cases, and then only with extremely violent inmates.[9]

The prison administration tried but failed to integrate these five sets of regulations into a single, national set of rules. Prison experts argued that the lack of similar standards of dress, diet, discipline, and hygiene for all inmates would limit efforts to modernize and unify the prison system. Indeed, Italy would wait some twenty years before a general set of regulations was finally completed.[10]

The attempt to adopt the Auburn system of prison discipline used in the penitentiaries of the Kingdom of Sardinia-Piedmont met with criticism, particularly in the Italian Senate. At the end of 1861, a proposal to construct a new penitentiary according to the Auburn system breezed through the Chamber of Deputies. Numerous senators, however, favored the Philadelphia system, which had been the system of prison discipline used in the Grand Duchy of Tuscany. As one senator noted, the construction of a new Auburn-style penitentiary before the issue of prison discipline had been thoroughly debated would establish "a dangerous precedent" for the future of the Italian prison system. Opponents in the Senate won a majority and refused to pass the bill.[11]

As a consequence of the dissent and opposition in the Senate, Bettino Ricasoli, the minister of the interior, established a bicameral commission to examine the prison question. Ricasoli named several notable advocates of prison reform in preunification Italy to the committee, including Carlo Peri of Tuscany and Giuseppe Minghelli-Vaini of Naples. But Piedmontese officials again dominated the eight-man committee.[12]

Ricasoli ordered the committee to study and answer a series of questions. Above all, the commission was to decide the proper system of prison discipline. The group was also assigned to examine the viability of the *bagni penali* and to consider whether or not the Ministry of the Interior should supersede the Ministry of the Navy in assuming the administration of them. Finally, the panel was asked to explore the viability of penal agricultural colonies in the Italian prison system.[13]

As evidenced by its final report, the committee supported the development of a prison system modeled after the Tuscan rather than the Piedmontese prison system. A majority favored, for example, the adoption of the Philadelphia system throughout Italy. Following the Tuscan precedent, the panel recommended the abolition of the *bagni penali*. Finally, the committee urged that the Ministry of the Interior administer all prisons and supported the use of penal agricultural colonies on a limited scale.[14]

The commission's report proved little more than an exercise in futility. Although all sides clamored for prison reform, political events in the South halted discussion on the report in either house of Parliament. Perhaps the most enduring aspect of the work of this early commission was its failure. Subsequent studies by later committees would likewise grind to a halt.[15]

The Italian Parliament did attempt to improve the material conditions of the custodial prisons, however. In 1864, both houses approved the extension of a Piedmontese law of 1857 that called for the construction of cellular custodial prisons in all major cities. It was argued that cellular isolation would improve hygiene and also facilitate the separation of inmates in the custodial prisons. This law was passed, but the government failed to provide the funds needed to construct the new cellular prisons. The recurring shortage of money would limit any real reform of the Italian prison system in ensuing decades. By the end of the decade, only three new custodial prisons were under construction.[16]

Difficulties in achieving the legislative unification of Italy also slowed prison reform during and after the 1860s. Here, too, the government followed a policy of "Piedmontization." Both the Piedmontese civil and penal codes were modified in 1859 in anticipation of a united Italy. Although several preunification states resisted the introduction of both codes, the Piedmontese civil code became the Italian civil code in 1865, with only slight modifications.[17]

The Piedmontese penal code of 1859 did not fare so well. Initially, the code met no opposition in the North and was rapidly extended to these provinces. In the South, the former Kingdom of the Two Sicilies accepted the penal code in 1861, but only after several revisions. The Tuscans, however, fiercely and unanimously objected to the introduction of the Piedmontese penal code in their former Grand Duchy of Tuscany. They insisted upon retaining the Tuscan penal code of 1853, which many Italian legal theorists considered the best of the preunification era. In particular, the Tuscans strongly opposed the reestablishment of the death penalty which had been abolished in Tuscany in 1859 but which continued to be a possibility under the Piedmontese penal code.[18]

Carlo Cattaneo, with his usual foresight, had predicted that the question of the death penalty would inhibit the legislative unification of Italy. In 1860, he maintained that no compromise would be possible on this issue. The death penalty must either be abolished throughout the country or reestablished in Tuscany. Cattaneo also anticipated that any proposal to eliminate the death penalty would become linked to the need for prison reform.[19]

Indeed, parliamentary officials, prison administrators, and journalists consistently argued that the death penalty should be abolished only if imprisonment could substitute as a punishment equal to the death penalty. In 1865, Deputy Pasquale Stanislao Mancini presented a proposal to the Chamber that would outlaw the death penalty throughout the peninsula and simultaneously extend the Piedmontese penal code to Tuscany. This same proposal also called for the study and implementation of prison reform in Italy.[20]

Mancini argued passionately against the death penalty in the parliamentary debates on his proposed law in February and March 1865. Clearly in the tradition of Beccaria, Mancini maintained that the death penalty no longer deterred crime and that it had become a "useless cruelty" that should be abolished.[21]

Several critics of Mancini's proposal balked at eliminating the death penalty before improvements were made in the Italian prison system. Vacca, the minister of justice, for example, stated that only extended cellular isolation or deportation could substitute for the death penalty. He argued that the death penalty could not be abolished without a program for the construction of more cellular prisons. Because such work would require careful and time-consuming planning, Vacca refused to support Mancini's proposal.[22]

The press of the day echoed Vacca's call for a massive overhaul of the Italian prison system. A widely read moderate newspaper, *L'Opinione* of Florence, pointed out that prisoners often escaped from Italy's relatively insecure prisons. The newspaper blamed the easily corrupted prison guards and the insufficient number of prison cells for the problem. Cellular prisons were considered particularly important because in them "the assassin finds himself alone, before God and his conscience, without the slightest hope that he can escape his punishment by corrupting the guards or by fleeing the prison." The editor of the newspaper asked the deputies to construct more cellular prisons and to improve the training of the guards before they voted to abolish the death penalty.[23]

These strongly expressed fears of mass escapes from Italian prisons were not unfounded. Between 1862 and 1865, escapes from all types of penal institutions numbered well over one thousand. The problem was especially acute in the custodial prisons where the inmates often fled in groups. In 1862, for example, 127 prisoners escaped *en masse* from the custodial prison of Girgenti in Sicily.[24]

The ongoing brigands' war in the South accounted for some of these mass escapes. Bands of brigands commonly opened prison doors and released all the inmates.[25] Indeed, Giuseppe Massari recognized in his official report on the conflict that "the ease of escaping is a great source of recruitment to brigandage."[26]

These arguments and statistics did not defeat Mancini's proposal in the Chamber of Deputies. On 16 March 1865, the Chamber chose to accept the measure by a vote of 127–96. One month later, however, the Senate voted against the proposed law. A number of senators tried but failed to pass a bill extending the death penalty to Tuscany.[27]

The collapse of Mancini's proposal effectively ended the possibility of extending the Piedmontese penal code to Tuscany.[28] Parliament decided, instead, to prepare a completely new penal code for the entire country. With this end in mind, the government established a new commission in November 1865 to examine the proper scale of punishments for the new penal code. This investigatory body, whose members included Giuseppe Boschi and Carlo Peri, essentially renewed the work of the earlier committees on prison reform. The eight-man panel was asked, for example, to decide upon the best system of prison discipline. It was also asked to explore the use of the *bagni penali*, the penal agricultural colonies, and the institution of parole in Italy. But this commission proved even less productive than its predecessor and failed to address most of these issues.[29]

The government therefore decided to link the agenda of this first committee to the work of a second one, appointed in January 1861. This second committee was a much larger investigatory body and was specifically instructed to draft a new penal code for Italy. After some debate, the panel decided to formulate a new penal system that excluded the death penalty. A majority of the commission then voted to substitute extended cellular isolation for the death penalty. Deportation was ruled out as an impractical and inexpensive alternative to the death penalty. The committee also argued against the use of parole, and it approved only limited use of penal agricultural colonies.[30]

An epidemic of cholera and the outbreak of the war of 1866 with Austria combined to halt the work of this investigatory body. By the end of the year, yet another project was presented to the same commission. This proposed penal code also ruled out the use of capital punishment and called for cellular isolation for a maximum of fifteen years. Although several members of the commission—most notably Mancini and Dr. Carlo Morselli—argued that such punishment could cause physical and mental harm to the prisoner, the commission voted to support this proposal. The minister of justice, however, appointed a subcommittee to examine this proposal; it advocated the use of the Auburn or congregate system instead of extended cellular isolation. In the final vote, the Auburn system won a majority in the committee. But this proposal would undergo further revisions and would not be presented to Parliament until the 1870s.[31]

As this new round of debates raged on, the prison system and prison administration again came under close scrutiny. In particular, Federico Bellazzi, a member of the committee set up in 1865, devoted his efforts to a thorough investigation of the Italian prison system. He had begun his work as early as 1864 when, as a deputy in the Chamber, he called for the creation of patronage societies to assist released juveniles and adults as they readjusted to society.[32]

As a consequence of his undeniable interest in prison reform, Bellazzi earned the position of vice president of the 1865 commission on penal reform. He tried but failed to extend the commission's work to include a comprehensive plan for the transformation of the Italian prison system. In 1866, however, he initiated his own plans for prison reform by publishing a highly critical study of the condition of Italian prisons.[33]

Bellazzi directed most of his criticism against the prison administration. Throughout his book, *Prigioni e prigionieri del regno d'Italia*, he seized every opportunity to accuse the prison administration of inertia and lack of imagination. For example, he began with an attack on the administration's attempt to explain away the mass escapes from Italian prisons. Bellazzi argued that the administration's claim that such escapes stemmed from the "unfortunate" material conditions of most Italian prisons was little more than a weak excuse for a major problem.[34] As he saw it, the prison administration needed to conduct extensive surveys and inquiries into the state of the Italian prisons and present those reports, along with requests for more money, to the Italian Parliament. Bellazzi was confident that the deputies would readily supply the money needed for prison reform if they understood the nature of the problem.[35]

Bellazzi also alleged that the prison administration seemed incapable of executing the 1864 law calling for the construction of cellular custodial prisons. He maintained that the prison bureaucracy spent more time planning projects than completing them. This slow response led Bellazzi to perceive "a certain hesitation, approaching inertia, which paralyzes and causes disorder and confusion in the administration."[36]

Like many other proponents of prison reform in Italy, Bellazzi argued that his country could learn a great deal from foreign experiences in prison organization and administration. He called for the compilation of annual reports on the condition of the prisons, including statistics on the prison population, "as is done in France, England, Belgium and other nations."[37] In the construction of new prisons, Bellazzi urged that Italy learn from the French experience and stop converting old convents and monasteries into prisons. He observed that the French had shown that such renovations of old buildings hindered rather than helped the creation of a modern prison system. Finally, Bellazzi called for the closing of the *bagni penali*—a step that had already been achieved in France in 1854.[38]

Throughout his work, Bellazzi offered several other suggestions to improve the Italian prison system. He again proposed, for example, the establishment of patronage societies to assist prisoners upon their release. He also argued that the director general of the prisons must be a vocal and public advocate of prison reform as well as a good administrator. Arguing that a link existed between literacy and crime, Bellazzi pleaded finally for an improvement in Italy's system of primary education.[39]

After the publication of his book, Bellazzi continued to voice in the Italian Parliament his concern and desire for prison reform. Claiming that he was interested in improving the Italian penal system for reasons of "social defense," he asked the minister of the interior to correct some of the more "urgent problems." In particular, he requested an explanation of the excessive number of juveniles in Milan's custodial prisons and the high mortality rate in Turin's prison for women.[40]

The minister of the interior offered only ambiguous responses to Bellazzi's inquiries. Indeed, he implied that Bellazzi's statistics and information were inaccurate and biased. When some other deputies proposed a complete reform of the prison system, with particular attention to the classification and separation of prisoners by offense and age, the minister claimed that he could not accept this proposal. Although he admitted that the prisons of Italy left much to be desired, he contended that the overcrowding resulted from "social evils" rather than from inadequacies in prison administration.[41]

A rising member of the prison administration, Martino Beltrani-Scalia, provided a more pointed response to Bellazzi's criticisms of the prison administration.[42] In a lengthy letter that was published in part in the official journal of the prison administration, *Effemeride carceraria,* Beltrani-Scalia, who was then prison inspector, accused Bellazzi of using outdated evidence and statistics from the preunification era. He also argued that Bellazzi overestimated the importance of building new, cellular prisons. He asserted that the mass escapes resulted most often because of the lack of well-trained guards:

> One may have prisons made of bronze. If the guards are bad, the prisoners will always escape. If one has instead a less than perfect prison but an intelligent, energetic, and conscientious prison director, and clever, moral, sober, and *incorruptible* prison guards, then, believe me, escapes will fall by ninety percent.[43]

Indeed, Beltrani-Scalia maintained that Italy's financial situation forced the prison administration to renovate old convents and monasteries instead of building new prisons.[44]

In the final analysis, however, Beltrani-Scalia could not dispute all of Bellazzi's findings. During the 1860s, the prison administration had achieved only limited reforms. The most heralded reform, the 1864 law requiring the construction of cellular custodial prisons, met with very limited success. The only other reform of the decade was the transfer of the administration of the *bagni penali* from the Ministry of the Navy to the Ministry of the Interior. But even this change was criticized because so many theorists wanted to eliminate the *bagni penali* entirely.[45]

Furthermore, conditions in the Neapolitan custodial prisons amply supported Bellazzi's criticisms. A board of inquiry, appointed by the Ministry of the Interior, reported in 1869 that the material conditions of the prisons of Naples had hardly improved since Gladstone's last visit in 1850. This investigatory body also declared that "all of these problems may be reduced to three major factors: the poor arrangement of the prisons, the excessive overcrowding, and the illegal mixing [of inmates]."[46] Among its recommendations, the Commission urged—like Bellazzi—the construction of new cellular prisons and classification of inmates according to age, sex, and offense.[47]

The available statistics on the Italian prison population also supported Bellazzi's conclusion that lack of education caused people to turn to a life of crime. A report in 1867 showed that more than 58 percent of all male prisoners and 62 percent of all female prisoners could neither read nor write. Of the eleven thousand inmates in the thirty-seven Italian penitentiaries, only 580 attended school while in prison.[48]

Despite these limited achievements, members of the Italian prison administration continued to propose grand schemes for a complete restructuring of the Italian prison system. In 1868, Giuseppe Minghelli-Vaini offered a number of suggestions for improvement in his work, *Sopra la riforma penitenziaria e sopra le spese occorrente per introdurla nel regno d'Italia.*[49] To lower costs, he proposed a reduction in the length of most sentences. He also urged the use of local doctors and priests in lieu of hiring permanent medical and religious personnel. Finally, he recommended the use of convict labor for public works outside the prison walls. He did think, however, that the prisoners should wear masks when working in public in order to eliminate any possible exchange between the public and the convicts.[50]

Minghelli-Vaini also recognized the need for a comprehensive reform of the Italian prison system. Echoing the trend of the day, he called for the introduction of either the English or Irish system of prison discipline. These eclectic systems, developed in the 1840s and 1850s by Joshua Jebb of England and Walter Crofton of Ireland, combined elements of the Auburn and Philadelphia systems of prison discipline. Both envisioned a three-stage process in which the prisoner would begin his sentence in a brief period of solitary confinement (nine months maximum). The inmate would then spend most of his sentence working in common with other prisoners by day and segregated in his cell by night. During this second stage, each prisoner could also gain privileges for good conduct. In the third stage, the prisoner could earn parole or a "ticket of leave." Prisoners under the Irish system, unlike the English system, would spend the third and final stage in an "intermediate prison" where they received further agricultural or industrial training in anticipation of their release. The inmates also heard lectures and advice on ways to avoid a life of crime once they were freed.[51]

Like Minghelli-Vaini, Beltrani-Scalia enthusiastically supported the Irish system. In 1868, he received an invitation from Walter Crofton to address the Congress of Social Scientists in Birmingham, England. In a speech entitled "On the Current State of the Italian Prison System," Beltrani-Scalia talked very little about the progress made in prison reform in Italy since unification. He actually devoted most of his time to a discussion of the Irish system. Clearly a disciple of Crofton, he proclaimed:

> Truly, it is this system which stops the rebirth of pernicious passions better than the others and inspires virtuous and moral sentiments in the heart of the prisoner. . . . Certainly, this system will not cure all social evils, nor does it pretend to correct all prisoners; but . . . it offers the ordinary criminal the chance to show his good intentions.[52]

Beltrani-Scalia then identified Boschi, Mancini, and Minghelli-Vaini as some of the more prominent Italians who, like him, wanted to see the Irish system implemented in Italy.[53]

But not all members of the Italian prison administration favored the Irish system. Napoleone Vazio, the editor of *Effemeride carceraria*, started a feud with

Beltrani-Scalia by attacking him in the pages of this journal. Vazio criticized Beltrani-Scalia's unhesitating support of the Irish system, depicting him as a disciple who worshiped "Croftonism." In Vazio's opinion, the Irish system was too theoretical to be practical. Furthermore, he suggested that the system had not been adopted on a wide scale and was more of a fad than anything else. He also claimed that Boschi and Mancini did not advocate the introduction of the system in Italy.[54]

Predictably, Vazio's criticisms prompted a quick response from Beltrani-Scalia. In a letter published in *Effemeride carceraria*, he expressed surprise that Vazio had found his speech unenlightening. After defending the merits of the Auburn system, he launched into a rather petty discussion of Vazio's translation of his speech. He ended the letter by implying that Vazio was behind the times and lacked understanding of the more modern theories of prison reform.[55]

This vituperative and essentially unproductive exchange between two prominent members of the Italian prison administration reflected the inadequate state of Italian prison reform at the end of the 1860s. Throughout the decade, the prison administration and the Italian Parliament had proposed various plans for prison reform. But in spite of all the debate and discussion, only minimal improvement had been achieved. Thus, at the end of the 1860s, the prison administration could give this dismal picture of the thirty-seven Italian penitentiaries:

> It is deplorable that only in a few penitentiaries can prison discipline be rigorously enforced. In most penitentiaries, it is impossible to enforce separation at night and the rule of silence. It is thus impossible to prevent immoral and corrupt exchanges between the inmates. Still another extremely grave problem is the inability of the penitentiaries to hold all 12,000 prisoners, a number greater than the number of places available. These convicts are thus forced to serve their sentences in the custodial prisons.[56]

The prison administration argued that these problems and similar ones in the 1,566 custodial prisons and the twenty-four *bagni penali* could easily be resolved if the government spent enough money on the prison system. More importantly, prison officials maintained that real prison reform could begin only after the new penal code was finished. No one seemed to anticipate that several decades would elapse before these basic requirements for penal reform would be realized.[57]

Notes

1. For more discussion of the political and administrative unification of Italy, see Harry Hearder, *Italy in the Age of the Risorgimento, 1790–1870* (London: Longman, 1983), 235–247; Denis Mack Smith, *Italy: A Modern History*, new and rev. ed. (Ann Arbor: University of Michigan Press, 1969), 27–59; and Giorgio Candeloro, *Storia dell'Italia moderna* (Milan: Feltrinelli, 1970), vol. 5, *La costruzione dello stato unitario*. It should also be noted that Victor Emmanuel II of the Kingdom of Sardinia-Piedmont, in a controversial move, chose to remain Victor Emmanuel II of the Kingdom of Italy.

2. The *bagni penali* remained under the authority of the Ministry of the Navy until 1867.

3. Ernesto Querci-Seriacopi, *Il passato, il presente, e l'avvento dell'amministrazione delle carceri in Italia* (Rome: Tip. delle Mantellate, 1925), 6–8; Beltrani-Scalia, *Sul governo e sulla riforma*, 481; and Napoleone Vazio, "Degli ispettori generali e centrali delle carceri," *Effemeride carceraria* (hereafter *E. C.*) (Florence) 2 (December 1866): 714–715.

4. Vazio, "Degli ispettori generali," 716–718.

5. Carlo Peri, for example, the former director general of the Tuscan prisons, was one of the first national prison inspectors.

6. Querci-Seriacopi, 7–8; and Vazio, "Degli ispettori generali," 718–726.

7. The full text of the *Regolamento generale per le carceri giudiziarie del regno* may be found in *E. C.* (Florence) 1 (January–September 1865): 237–244, 293–304, 355–360, 413–422, 489–494, and 551–568.

8. These penal institutions included custodial prisons (*carceri giudiziarie*), the penitentiaries (*case di pena*), the juvenile prisons *(case di custodia)*, the *case di relegazione*, the *bagni penali*, and the penal colony on the island of Pianosa. Regulations for each of these establishments were issued between 1861–1863. See Beltrani-Scalia, *Sul governo e sulla riforma*, 481.

9. This point was brought out in a 1865 during a discussion in Parliament. The director of the penitentiary of Parma had violated these regulations in 1865 when he approved the use of a straitjacket on a rebellious inmate. See "Interpellanza del Deputato Bellazzi," *E. C.* (Florence) 3 (June 1867): 54–55; "La tortura in Italia," *Il Conciliatore*, 18 February 1867; and "Cronaca," *E. C.* (Florence) 3 (June 1867): 76–77.

10. New regulations for the Italian prison system were completed in 1889.

11. Beltrani-Scalia, *Sul governo e sulla riforma*, 482.

12. Ibid., 483–484.

13. Ibid., 484–485.

14. Ibid., 489–499. The Tuscan *bagni penali* were closed in 1850. Tuscany also pioneered the use of a penal agricultural colony on the island of Pianosa.

15. Ibid., 505–506.

16.   A later advocate of prison reform, Giuseppe Minghelli-Vaini, estimated that Italy needed to construct some 43,000 cells in order to fulfill the requirements of this law. But these new prisons took years to complete. Construction of the custodial prison "Le Nuove" in Turin, for example, began in 1862 after five years of planning and preparation. The prison was finally opened in 1869. See Giuseppe Minghelli-Vaini, "Sopra la riforma penitenziaria e sopra le spese occorrente per introdurla nel regno d'Italia," *E. C.* (Florence) 4 (August 1868): 465–497; Vera Comoli Mandracci and Giovanni Maria Lupo, *Il carcere giudiziario di Torino detto "Le Nuove"* (Turin: Centro studi piemontesi, 1974); and Federico Bellazzi, *Prigioni e prigionieri nel regno d'Italia* (Florence: Tip.   G.   Barbera, 1866), 14–16.

17.   For a complete discussion of the revision of the Piedmontese civil code, see Alberto Aquarone, *L'unificazione legislativa e i codici del 1865* (Milan: Dott.   A.   Giuffrè, 1960), 5–23.

18.   In the South, for example, the penalty against perjury was eliminated. For the other modifications, see Pessina, *Il diritto penale in Italia*, II: 649–654; and Aquarone, 89–97.

19.   Carlo Cattaneo, *Scritti politici*, ed.   Mario Boneschi (Florence: Le Monnier, 1964), I: 400–407.

20.   The text of Mancini's proposal is printed in Aquarone, *L'unificazione*, 321–322.

21.   These debates may also be found in ibid., 322–337.

22.   Ibid., 337–342.

23.   This article, dated 14 March 1865, is reprinted in ibid., 348–349.

24.   See "Sulle evasioni dalle carceri," *E.   C.* (Florence) 1 (August and October, 1865): 449–469, 577–597; Bellazzi, *Prigioni e prigionieri*, 84–96; and "Ancora sulle evasioni dalle carceri," *E.   C.* (Florence) 2 (August and September 1866): 449–461, 511–525.

25.   For a thorough discussion of the brigands' war, consult Franco Molfese, *Storia del brigantaggio dopo l'Unità* (Milan: Feltrinelli, 1966).

26.   Quoted in Mack Smith, *Italy*, 74–75. The Pica Law of 1863 authorized the government to use residential confinement *(domicilio coatto)* in response to the brigands' war. A person could be sentenced without trial to *domicilio coatto* for a maximum of one year. Provisions for *domicilio coatto* were included in the Public Security Law of 1865. Residential confinement continued to be used after the suppression of the brigands' war. Some historians argue that it provided a cheap alternative to imprisonment. For further information, see Davis, *Conflict and Control*, 217; and Richard Bach Jensen, "Liberty and Order: The Theory and Practice of Italian Public Security Policy," (Ph. D. diss., University of Minnesota, 1983), 41–47.

27.   Aquarone, *L'unificazione legislativa*, 31–33, 353–361.

28.   Until a new penal code was completed in 1888, Tuscany retained its penal code of 1853 with the provision of 1860 abolishing the death penalty.

29. For the decree establishing the commission, see *E. C.* (Florence) 1 (November 1865): 659–661. See also "Commissione governativa per la riforma delle prigioni del regno," *E. C.* (Florence) 2 (February 1866): 65–68; and Martino Beltrani-Scalia, *La riforma penitenziaria in Italia* (Rome: Tip. Artero, 1879), 18–22.

30. This second commission included Francesco Carrara and Enrico Pessina, two of Italy's most distinguished legal theorists. For a list of all members, see *E. C.* (Florence) 2 (January 1866):   40–41.

31. Beltrani-Scalia, *La riforma penitenziaria,* 25–28.

32. Born in Milan in 1825, Bellazzi pursued legal studies at the University of Pavia and the University of Turin. A participant in the 1848 uprising in Milan, Bellazzi also supported Garibaldi in 1860. After unification, Bellazzi was elected to the Chamber of Deputies in 1863. His promising career was cut short in 1868 when he committed suicide in Florence. For more information, see Pietro Dal Canto, *Biografia di Federico Bellazzi* (Florence: Tip. Bonducciana di C. Alessandri, 1869).

33. Beltrani-Scalia, *La riforma penitenziaria,* 20–22.

34. Bellazzi was specifically responding to a series of articles published in *E. C.* in 1865. See above, note 24.

35. Bellazzi, *Prigioni e prigionieri,* 3–10.

36. Ibid., 14.

37. Ibid., 8.

38. Ibid., 127–145.

39. Ibid., 150–151.

40. Ibid., 67–69.

41. Ibid.

42. It is not surprising that Beltrani-Scalia led the attack on Bellazzi. The son of Vito Beltrani, Beltrani-Scalia was born in 1829 in Palermo. Expelled from Sicily after the revolutions of 1848, he spent time in London and Paris. He began to work on a history of the Italian prison system as early as 1855 and published it in 1868. He continued to write on topics related to prison reform until his death in 1909. Beltrani-Scalia also rose rapidly in the Italian prison administration and will figure prominently in next chapters of this study. For more information on his life and career, see Martino Beltrani-Scalia, *Rivoluzione di Sicilia* (*Memorie storiche*), ed. G. P. F. Beltrani (Rome: M. Tupini, 1933), I: 5–50.

43. "La lettera di Beltrani-Scalia," *E. C.* (Florence) 3 (March 1867): 158–159.

44. Ibid., 144–145.

45. For the decree ordering the transfer, see *E. C.* (Florence) 3 (January 1867):   105–106.

46. "Relazione della commissione d'inchiesta sulle carceri giudiziarie di Napoli," *E. C.* (Florence) 5 (August 1869):   488.

47. Ibid., 400–405.

48. Giuseppe Sacchi, "Uno sguardo alla popolazione carceraria del regno d'Italia," *E. C.* (Florence) 3 (June 1867): 365–372.

49. Minghelli-Vaini began his career in the Piedmontese prison system as the director of the penitentiary at Oneglia. He consistently opposed the Philadelphia system. As a member of the 1862 commission, for example, he had dissented from the majority's support of extended cellular isolation and had argued that the Auburn system was cheaper to implement and also better for the health of the inmates. See his early assessment of the two systems in his work, *Sulla riforma delle carceri e l'assistenza pubblica* (Turin: G. Bocca, 1852), I: 20-21.

50. Minghelli-Vaini, "Sopra la riforma," 236–254.

51. Ibid., 345. For further information on the English and Irish systems, see Mary Carpenter, *Reformatory Prison Discipline, as developed by the Rt. Hon. Sir Walter Crofton, in the Irish Convict Prisons* (London: Longman, Longman and Green, 1872); and Beverly Ann Smith, "The Irish Prison System, 1854–1914: Prisons and Political Prisoners" (Ph.D. diss., Miami University, Ohio, 1977), especially 28–33.

52. Napoleone Vazio, "Le prigioni italiane dinanzi al Congresso di Scienze Sociali a Birmingham," *E. C.* (Florence) 5 (January 1869): 15.

53. Ibid., 16–17. It should be noted that Beltrani-Scalia dedicated his work, *Sul governo e sulla riforma delle carceri in Italia* (1868), to Sir Walter Crofton.

54. Ibid., 18–38.

55. "Le prigioni italiane dinanzi al Congresso di Scienze Sociali a Birmingham," *E. C.* (Florence) 5 (February and March 1869): 131–172.

56. "Condizioni attuali delle prigioni in Italia," *E. C.* (Florence) 5 (February and March 1869): 85.

57. Ibid., 82–89.

4

The Limits of Prison Reform, 1870–1887

The pattern of inaction and inertia that characterized Italian prison reform in the 1860s continued during the next two decades. Throughout this period, the financial problems of the newly unified liberal kingdom seriously limited the amount of money available for the Italian prison system. In the early 1870s, the leaders of the still politically dominant Right (*Destra*) and prison administration officials searched for ways to reduce the cost of the prison system without undertaking a comprehensive program of prison reform. After the Left (*Sinistra*) gained control of the government in 1876, the director general of the prisons, Martino Beltrani-Scalia, encouraged by the Left and especially by Francesco Crispi, laid the groundwork for a complete renovation of the prison system. But even then, financial problems slowed the realization of his proposals. And the emergence of the positive school of criminology further called his ideas into question.

The drive to limit expenditure on the Italian prison system in the 1870s was directly linked to the financial policies of the Right. The Right's favorite minister of finance, Quintino Sella, practiced an austere policy of "economy to the bone" in an effort to eliminate the huge deficit that had emerged after the war with Austria in 1866. This determination to balance the budget touched all aspects of Italian life. Appropriations for the military and plans for educational reform were reduced or cut as a consequence. To obtain quick cash, former church lands were sold to private speculators. The government also introduced new taxes, most notably the hated grist tax (*macinato*), in its attempts to fill the coffers of the Treasury.[1]

It is thus not surprising that most of the debates on prison reform, especially during the last years of the era of the Right, revolved around ways to reduce the cost of the prison system without promoting an increase in crime. The numerous suggestions ranged from streamlining the prison bureaucracy to the outright abolition of the prison system. Although many of the proposals were ultimately rejected, they absorbed the time and attention of the Italian Right and the prison bureaucracy and further limited any real improvement of the prison system.

Transportation (i.e., deportation to a remote penal colony) was one of the most widely discussed alternatives to the penitentiary. Inspired by the example of England and France,[2] Italians claimed that penal colonies would reduce crime and also cost the government less than the prison system. Even though the earlier parliamentary committees on prison reform and the penal code (1862 and 1865) had argued effectively against the use of transportation, the notion that it was the ideal solution to Italy's crime problem refused to die. In 1866, for example, Biagio Caranti of the Ministry of Agriculture and Commerce contended that Italian public opinion favored transportation, particularly given the condition of Italian public security. He urged the creation of a penal colony in the Indian Ocean where Italy could deposit its unwanted criminal population and also enjoy "a certain prestige and renown."[3]

This promise of an inexpensive and perhaps prestigious solution to Italy's acute crime problem appealed to the government. In the annual report on the budget for 1870, the Ministry of the Interior predicted that the use of deportation would cost the government less per year. More importantly, it would permit the closure of those "havens of vice and crime," the *bagni penali*.[4] Encouraged by these claims, the government authorized the Ministry of the Navy and the foreign secretary to begin a search for a suitable location for a penal colony, preferably in the Indian Ocean.[5]

The government's study of deportation had the full support of Emilio Cerruti and Count Adolfo DeForesta. Cerruti, for example, penned several articles on the topic for popular and widely read journals like *Nuova Antologia*. He maintained that a comprehensive reform of Italy's prison system would require years of work and millions of lire. Transportation was, in his judgment, the only viable solution to Italy's crime problem. He contended that Italy, once purged of its "incorrigible criminals," would enjoy an unprecedented decline in crime and eventually see the disappearance of criminal organizations like the mafia and the *camorra*. A penal colony would also give Italy a strategic position in other parts of the globe. Furthermore, both ex-convicts and free citizens would be able to begin their life anew without any stigma or shame. Cerruti thus advocated the creation of penal colonies in the Melanesian Islands, similar to the English penal colonies in Australia.[6]

Count Adolfo DeForesta shared Cerruti's enthusiasm for transportation. He too believed that Italy's prison system was in shambles and would cost a fortune to renovate. He also showed no sympathy for the promise that the cellular prison—that "barbarous American invention"—could reform and rehabilitate the criminal. Indeed, he maintained that cellular isolation simply gave a prisoner the time to dream about his revenge. DeForesta therefore called for the abolition of all prisons except for the custodial prison.

De Foresta advocated the establishment of three types of penal colonies to replace the penitentiary. The first category of colony, to be located somewhere outside the Mediterranean Sea, would house criminals convicted of major crimes like homicide. These criminals would be given a sentence of permanent deportation and never be allowed to return to Italy. The second type of colony, to be located in the Mediterranean Sea or Adriatic Sea, would accommodate criminals convicted of severe crimes without a life sentence. In the colony, each inmate would be required to perform several years of hard labor. Inmates with good conduct records would be permitted to work on the Italian peninsula in land reclamation projects or in the construction of railroads. The last variety of colony, agricultural colonies located within the Italian peninsula, would be reserved for criminals sentenced to less than three years.[7]

Officials in the Italian prison administration, perhaps because they were concerned about their future employment, did not display the same eagerness to introduce transportation. In particular, a well-known official in the prison administration, Martino Beltrani-Scalia, threw his considerable weight against the idea. In an effort to silence the popular debate on the merits of transportation, he directly attacked both Cerruti and De Foresta in his work, *La deportazione* (1874).

Beltrani-Scalia objected to transportation for both philosophical and economic reasons. Unlike Cerruti and De Foresta, he clearly believed in the reformative possibilities of the prison. He argued that with the proper dosage of surveillance, education, and labor, a prisoner could leave the penitentiary a changed man. He conceded that the Italian prison system was notoriously inadequate to the task; but, with time and effort, the system could be improved and criminals remade into honest men.

Beltrani-Scalia cited statistics and evidence from the English and French experience to prove that transportation would prove more costly than a comprehensive reform of the prison system. These same statistics also revealed that transportation did not reduce crime nor eliminate recidivism. Beltrani-Scalia also contended that transportation was immoral and inhumane because it separated prisoners from their homeland and families. In sum, he maintained that transportation was a punishment whose time had passed and was certainly not the miraculous cure to crime that Italy hoped for.[8]

In the end, Beltrani-Scalia's views prevailed, largely because the government determined that transportation would indeed be costly. The fact-finding missions of the early 1870s reaped little reward.[9] In the annual report on the budget of the Ministry of the Interior, Antonio Di Rudinì concluded:

> If deportation is an ineffective financial adventure, we cannot readily support it in Italy where the financial question precedes all other questions, and where we lack the indispensable naval

forces to maintain a remote empire, and where we even lack the colonies required for such an experiment.[10]

Government officials also saw the steady employment of Italy's fifty thousand or so inmates as a practical and painless way to lower the cost of the prison system. Advocates of prison reform had long supported work in prison as an essential aspect of a rehabilitative program. Prison officials had sought to ensure that this labor was productive and prepared inmates to support themselves by honest means after their release from prison. Therefore, they encouraged industrial work and rejected such unproductive and punitive labor as the treadmill and the shot drill.[11]

Once the idea of prison labor was accepted, the question arose how best to manage it so that it would yield the highest profit margin. In the 1860s, the Italian government sponsored all industrial labor performed in the penitentiaries and *bagni*. Under the system of state management, the state purchased all of the required raw materials and equipment, and the prison director and his assistants supervised the work of the inmates. This method permitted the prison director to control the work of his inmates, but its several disadvantages included the cost of the work materials and the business skills demanded of the prison director.[12]

In response to the expenses and disadvantages of state management, the Italian government began to experiment with the contract system of prison labor after 1868. This system involved contracting out the labor of the prisoners in a given institution to the lowest bidder. The state fed and clothed the prisoners while the contractor supplied all of the materials needed for industrial production. Advocates of the system argued that it was cheaper than state management because the state was not required to pay for the raw material, machines, and the training of personnel.[13]

Initially, the contract system impressed prison officials favorably. At the International Prison Congress in London in 1872, Felice Cardon, the director general of the prisons, noted that eleven of Italy's thirty-five penitentiaries were experimenting with this system.[14] Other prison officials similarly asserted that discipline was better under the contract system because it freed the prison director from concern over prison labor and permitted him and his staff to devote their attention to the moral education and rehabilitation of each inmate.[15]

The contract system did result in more work for prisoners and a higher profit margin for the Italian prison system.[16] But the very success of the system led to some thorny disputes between the prison administration and free labor. Free workers saw prison labor as unfair competition that artificially lowered the prices of their goods. In 1874, for example, the cobblers of Alessandria presented a petition to Parliament objecting to the contract system. In particular, the cobblers protested that the contractor should not be permitted to sell his goods in the city center. Even though the minister of the interior, Girolamo Cantelli, refused to revise the contracts between the prisons and the industrialists to limit the places where prison-made goods could be sold, the free workers remained undaunted and repeatedly objected to the contract system in ensuing years.[17]

The poor material conditions of Italy's penitentiaries also worked against the success of the contract system. The minister of the interior, Giovanni Lanza, lamented this difficulty in a parliamentary discussion in 1874. He maintained that it would cost the country a small fortune to adapt the prisons for industrial work:

> These are old convents, old government buildings, and old castles which were converted to prisons. It is thus difficult to adapt these buildings in ways suitable for industrial work.[18]

Both the inadequate buildings and the struggle with free labor would persist and leave the government searching for other ways to keep its large prison population employed.

The Right also stepped up its use of residential confinement (*domicilio coatto*) in the 1870s in an effort to reduce the cost of the prison system without compromising law and order. This method of crime prevention was less expensive than imprisonment because the government was not obligated to employ or maintain the confinees (*coatti*). In the wake of a series of tax riots and the Paris Commune of 1871, the Right pushed through new public security legislation which led to a dramatic rise in the number of persons sentenced to *domicilio coatto* (up from 573 in 1871 to 1,302 in 1872). These high numbers persisted until the collapse of the Right in March 1876, giving the government a sense of security without high expenditure.[19]

The occasional use of amnesty also provided the government with another easy method of reducing the prison population and the cost of the prison system. In 1869, for example, most of the men accused of participating in the grist tax riots were released.[20] The king also granted amnesty on special occasions. Upon his accession to the throne in 1878, for example, Umberto I released a variety of political prisoners and prisoners sentenced to less than six months. He also reduced most other sentences by an average of six months.[21]

Amnesty by itself could not eliminate the excessive number of inmates in Italy's various prisons. The overcrowding was particularly acute in the custodial prisons. According to the Criminal Procedure Code of 1863, the government was obliged to hold anyone suspected of criminal behavior or accused of a felony in a custodial prison without bail.[22] As the judicial system bogged down in the late 1860s, some inmates found themselves awaiting trial for more than a year. By the end of 1871, 28,293 of 46,587 inmates in the custodial prisons were still awaiting trial.[23]

Parliamentary deputies on both the Right and the Left lamented the expenses involved in keeping the accused in prison for such lengthy periods. Speaking for the Ministry of the Interior in 1875, Di Rudinì suggested revisions in the policy of preventive detention as a way to "apply the brakes" to spending on the prison system.[24]   But the calls for reform yielded no results. In the wake of perceived anarchist threats, the Italian government extended rather than limited the use of preventive detention.[25]

Indeed, for reasons of security, the Right attempted to improve the quality and discipline of the prison guards. Thus, in 1873, the government reorganized the guards into a military-style corps. The new regulations stipulated that an applicant to the corps undergo both physical and written examinations. Exempted from military service so long as they were prison guards, they nevertheless remained subject to the Military Penal Code. They were enrolled for an initial period of eight years, and promotions were based upon seniority. In order to promote an esprit de corps, the guards were required to live in a barracks and were not allowed to marry.[26] At the same time, the government authorized the creation of a training school for applicants to the corps of prison guards.[27]

But the cost of this reform also met with opposition in Parliament. Some deputies objected to spending money on the prison guards prior to an amelioration of the material conditions of the prisons. Supporters of the proposal, including Giuseppe Lanza, the minister of the interior, argued that the quality of the guards had to be improved for security reasons, especially to help prevent escapes. This argument finally won the day.[28]

Both the minister of the interior and Di Rudinì also suggested the extended use of parole for long-term prisoners as a way to reduce the number of prisoners in the penitentiaries.[29]   Although the governments of the Right made an effort to initiate this reform, the balance of power in the Parliament shifted to the Left before their work was completed. But the new minister of the interior, Giovanni Nicotera, introduced in Parliament a proposed law for parole on 23 May 1876. He urged its introduction both as a way to reduce the prison budget and as a way to help rehabilitate the prisoner. After some debate, the measure was passed in both houses and helped to reduce the prison budget.[30]

It is perhaps symbolic that the Italian Left managed to achieve a reform that had eluded the Right. After the *Sinistra* rose to power in 1876, Italian politics changed considerably. Even though Prime Minster Agostino Depretis and his cabinet confronted similar financial problems, they showed greater willingness to sponsor needed political and social reforms, such as changes in the voting rights and improvements in the prison system.[31]

Certain members of the Left, notably Francesco Crispi, demonstrated a marked interest in prison reform. During the annual discussion of the prison budget in 1879, Crispi accused the leaders of the Right of having used Italy's financial difficulties to avoid the resolution of the prison question. He maintained that the lack of money could slow but should not stop prison reform:

> The question of money should not frighten us. Introduce in the Chamber a plan for a comprehensive reform of the prison system, make a precise budget,. . . and after ten or twelve years, we will have obtained something we will never have unless we begin.[32]

Crispi then went on to argue, much to the chagrin of the *Destra*, that unless reforms were introduced, the Italian prisons would remain the seedbeds of crime that they had been since unification. He further contended that this reform was in the best financial interests of the state since more criminals meant more expenses.[33]

Crispi himself had initiated a comprehensive program of prison reform during his brief tenure as minster of the interior (December 1877–March 1878).[34] Almost immediately after coming to office, he had ordered the prominent prison official, Beltrani-Scalia, to submit a program for general reform that would be inexpensive and yet easy to implement.[35] After his departure from office, Crispi was named the president of a committee appointed in 1879 to consider the viability of Beltrani-Scalia's suggestions.[36] Even though this committee accomplished nothing, Beltrani-Scalia's work, *La riforma penitenziaria in Italia* (1879), laid the foundations for a complete renovation of the Italian prison system. Indeed, Beltrani-Scalia would realize some of his proposals after 1879 in his capacity as director general of the prisons.[37]

As previously noted, Beltrani-Scalia confidently believed in the reformative possibilities of the prison. Like most proponents of the classical school of criminology, he saw criminal behavior as the product of an improper environment. In the science of punishment, the objective was thus to create a proper environment in an institutional setting in which the criminal could be remade into an honest and productive member of society.[38]

Like many earlier advocates of prison reform, Beltrani-Scalia argued that the reform of Italy's prison system must begin in the custodial prisons. He portrayed these prisons as breeding grounds of crime, primarily because the hardened criminal was allowed to associate with the young first offender. Repeating the pleas of several parliamentary deputies,[39] Beltrani-Scalia called for the final implementation of the 1864 law that required the construction of cellular custodial prisons in all major cities. To minimize the cost of constructing the approximately forty thousand required cells, he suggested a reduction in the number of custodial prisons and urged that the design of the new prisons be simple and free from expensive architectural flourishes.[40]

Echoing his earlier works on prison reform, Beltrani-Scalia again called for the introduction of the Irish or Progressive system of prison discipline for long-term prisoners. An inmate would first spend up to one-fifth of his sentence in a penitentiary in complete cellular isolation. Depending on his conduct and his crime,[41] the prisoner would then be permitted to move to an intermediate prison, where he would be allowed to work in common with other inmates. Discipline in the second stage would also be more lenient. After completing no less than four-fifths of his sentence, and again depending on his conduct record, a prisoner would become eligible for the third stage, parole.[42]

Beltrani-Scalia asserted that the introduction of the Irish system would reap many benefits for Italy. It would ensure a more individualized treatment of each prisoner without eliminating the punitive nature of the prison.[43] Economically, it would save Italy money because fewer prisons would be required, prisoners would spend less time in cells, and the work of the prisoners would offset the cost of their maintenance.[44]

To ensure the profitability of prison labor, Beltrani-Scalia called for several changes in the employment of prisoners. He was strongly opposed to the contract system of prison labor, primarily because he saw the contractors as greedy speculators who were more interested in money than in rehabilitation of the inmates. He also questioned the type of industrial labor performed in Italy's penitentiaries and maintained that most prisoners reaped no long-term benefits from making matchboxes, for example. Furthermore, he argued that many of Italy's prisoners remained idle for most of their sentence and must therefore be put to work.[45]

Noting that most of Italy's prisoners were formerly either agricultural laborers or construction workers, Beltrani-Scalia urged the employment of the idle prisoners in a variety of public works:

> When I see that we need to build or renovate almost all of our prisons—or to build a line of railroad track on which we will spend almost a miliardo—or half of the peninsula in which we lack passable roads . . . or our ports to build—or better than 230 hectares of land to reclaim. . . . When I think of all these works which need to be done, and which everyone recognizes as urgent and useful, I ask myself: how can we leave so many individuals in idleness?[46]

Beltrani-Scalia further pointed out that Italy prisoners had been successfully employed in public works in other parts of the world. He thus maintained that the use of prisoners in these types of public works would help alleviate the costs of the prison system and also keep the idle prisoners active.[47]

Beltrani-Scalia stressed the need for a series of institutions and organizations that would "complement" the prison, as well. He particularly wanted to see patronage societies for released prisoners and juveniles established in all major cities. These patronage societies would assist former prisoners as they made the transition to the real world. He also hoped that the government would authorize extended use of parole so that prisoners would have the hope of an early release, even if they had received a lengthy sentence.[48]

To implement these proposed reforms, Beltrani-Scalia called for the creation of a highly centralized prison administration. The director general of the prisons would oversee the entire system. A series of regional or district inspectors would be the "eyes" of the prison administration and make annual reports of their inspection of all prisons. To ensure their dedication and suitability for the prison administration, all employees would be subjected to a rigorous examination process prior to entry into the prison service.[49]

Beltrani-Scalia's proposal to create district inspectors was quickly implemented. In 1881, a royal decree authorized the creation of six district inspectors. Centered in Rome after 1884, the six districts were established in Genoa, Florence, Rome, Messina, Naples, and Verona. Each inspector was ordered to scrutinize the buildings, personnel, and inmates of every prison within the district. In a statement that preceded the decree, Beltrani-Scalia declared that these inspectors would make the prison administration more efficient and also guarantee that all personnel did their duty.[50] Armed with official questionnaires, these inspectors began their work in 1881.[51]

Beltrani-Scalia's suggestion to employ prisoners in public works also bore fruit in the 1880s. Thus, in 1880, prisoners from the *bagni* of Civitavecchia and Orbetello were employed on an experimental basis in a land reclamation project that was supervised by the Trappist monks of Tre Fontane. The expense of the project and some early escapes were discouraging. Nevertheless, work continued in the colony. Within a year, another colony was established at Ponte Buttero. By 1883, the more than 373 prisoners working on the reclamation of the Roman *campagna* were cultivating some 148 hectares of reclaimed land.[52]

Parliamentary deputies overwhelmingly applauded these early efforts. The Ministry of the Interior reported in its annual budget proposal that Tre Fontane showed that using prisoners for public works "better responds to financial needs, better reaches the education and moral redemption of the prisoners."[53] And during the general discussion of the prison budget, many deputies praised the colony and suggested other types of public works in which prisoners could be profitably employed.[54]

Not all deputies supported the colony without question, however. In 1883, Corrado Tommasi-Crudeli interrogated the Ministry of the Interior on the sanitary conditions in the colony, particularly in light of the high mortality rate among both prisoners and guards during the summer months.[55] He then called for the closing of the colony during the summer months. His request was ignored, however, as Deputy Teodorico Bonacci and the minister of the interior both assured the Chamber that the current high death rate was atypical of the laudable experiment at Tre Fontane.[56]

Several popular journals shared Tommasi-Crudeli's reservations about the employment of prisoners in land reclamation projects. The *Rassegna settimanale*, for example, maintained that the costs of transport, housing, and extra guards made the colony of Tre Fontane more expensive than new penitentiaries. Like Tommasi-Crudeli, the journal also questioned the morality and legality of allowing prisoners to work in unhealthy locations, particularly during the summer months. Another critic, Leone Carpi, writing in the newspaper *Il popolo romano*, asserted that the use of prisoners in agricultural projects such as Tre Fontane forced free agricultural laborers to emigrate in search of employment. He argued that the *forzati* should be deported and put to work on remote islands.[57]

In response to these criticisms, Beltrani-Scalia defended the colony, asserting that it and other public works cost the prison administration 50 percent less than other types of work. He also argued that most prisoners were more suited for agricultural than industrial work.[58] A district inspector, Aristide Bernabo-Silorata, similarly maintained that well over 70 percent of Italy's prisoners had been employed in some sort of agricultural work before their imprisonment. Consequently, he argued, "they do not have, with few exceptions, any advantage from learning industrial skills during their imprisonment, because they almost always return to their previous occupation upon release." They must therefore be permitted to refine their agricultural skills during their imprisonment so that they would not be compelled to return to a life of crime upon release.[59]

The criticisms of parliamentary deputies and others did not bring to a halt the use of inmates in public works outside of the prison. By 1884, some 3,690 inmates from the *bagni penali* and the penitentiaries were employed in a variety of projects, including land reclamation in the Roman *campagna* and the construction of fortifications for both the army and navy. Prisoners were also used to build new prisons, most notably the new custodial prison in Rome, *Regina Coeli*.[60]

Beltrani-Scalia also enjoyed several other successes during his years as director general. Encouraged by Depretis, several cities initiated patronage societies for released prisoners and juveniles.[61] New regulations were written for the agricultural penal colonies.[62] The prison administration was also reorganized in 1887. And Beltrani-Scalia, inspired by the positivist spirit of the age, continued work on his favorite project, the compilation of statistics on the Italian prison system.[63]

But even though some of Beltrani-Scalia's proposals met with success, financial problems continued to limit any real improvement in the material conditions of Italy's prisons. Lack of money particularly slowed the construction of the cellular custodial prisons. In 1879, for example, after six years of postponement, the government delayed the construction of a new custodial prison in Rome "so as not to aggravate the State's budget."[64] Construction of the prison was resumed at last in the mid-1880s, with prisoners being used to build the prison.

Lack of money caused similar delays in the erection of new custodial prisons in all parts of Italy. In 1878, for example, Deputy Agostino Tumminelli implored Parliament to authorize the construction of a new custodial prison in Caltanissetta, Sicily. He stated that the current prison was unhealthy and that the city had been forced to house some inmates in a nearby public school.[65] Yet nothing was done. Six years later, the prefect of Caltanissetta noted that part of the custodial prison had collapsed. Indeed, he declared that "it is deplorable that the financial situation of our country does not permit us to think about the construction of the single new prison that everyone in this town sees as a real necessity."[66]

The district inspectors discovered a similarly bleak situation throughout the country. Giuseppe Berardi, inspector of the first district of Genoa, found that twenty-five of thirty-two custodial prisons were generally poorly maintained and unsanitary. Furthermore, the prisoners struck him as undisciplined and restless, and inmates were separated according to age, sex, and crime in only four of thirty-two prisons. In all other custodial prisons, he observed that "the convicted mixed with the accused, the military prisoners mixed with the civilian prisoners, and the adults mixed with the juveniles."[67]

The administrative personnel of the prison, as well as the prison guards, also contributed to the inefficient operation of Italy's prisons. During the 1880s, the prison guards regularly complained about their poor working conditions and extended working hours.[68] In a circular to all prison directors, dated 12 June 1882, Beltrani-Scalia warned the prison directors not to entrust the safety of their penitentiary to the corps of guards. He called upon the prison directors to help eliminate escapes by frequently visiting the prison. He also ordered each director to increase his personal surveillance of the prisoners who worked outside to make sure that the guards were neither beating the inmates nor permitting them to do as they pleased.[69]

Given this situation, it is not surprising that King Umberto I could declare in 1887 that Italy still required a comprehensive reform of its prison system. He, like many Italians, anticipated that such reform would accompany the impending approval of the unified penal code.[70]

Notes

1.   For a discussion of Italy's financial situation during this period, see Christopher Seton-Watson, *Italy from Liberalism to Fascism, 1870–1925* (New York: Methuen, 1967), 18–22; and Giorgio Candeloro, *Storia dell'Italia moderna* (Milan: Feltrinelli, 1970), vol. 6, *Lo sviluppo del capitalismo e del movimento operaio*, especially 68–84.

2.   England first used transportation in 1718, France in the 1790s. For more information on the English experience, see A. Roger Ekirch, *Bound for America* (Oxford: Clarendon Press, 1987). On France, see Gordon Wright, *Between the Guillotine and Liberty* (New York: Oxford University Press, 1983), especially 138–152.

3.   Biagio Caranti, "Una colonia penitenziaria," *L'Opinione* (Florence) 19, no. 313 (13–16 Nov. 1866): 1–2.

4.   See "Frammento della relazione della commissione parlamentare sul bilancio passivo del Minstero dell'Interno per l'esercizio 1870," *E.C.* (Florence) 6 (1870): 154–226, especially 195–199.

5.   "Sulla deportazione: Interrogazione del Senatore Caccia e risposta dell'on. Ministero di Grazia e Giustizia nella tornata del 17 dicembre 1872," *Rivista di discipline carceraria* (Rome) (hereafter *RDC*) 2 1872: 605–607.

6.   Emilio Cerruti, "Le colonie penali e le colonie libere," *Nuova antologia* 23 (July 1873): 673–722.

7.   Adolfo De Foresta, *Nè patibolo nè carcere* (Bologna: Nicola Zanichelli, 1880). De Foresta voiced similar opinions at the First International Prison Congress, held in London in 1872. See *Prisons and Reformatories at Home and Abroad, Being the Transactions of the International Penitentiary Congress* ed. Edwin Pears (London: Longman and Green and Co., 1872), 403–414.

8.   Martino Beltrani-Scalia, *La deportazione* (Rome: Tip. Artero and Comp., 1874).

9.   "Sulla deportazione," 605–607. See also the negative assessment of transportation by an Italian naval captain in *RDC* 4 (1874): 559–64.

10.   "Atti parlamentari," *RDC* 3 (1873): 513.

11.   These types of labor were common in English penitentiaries.

12.   See "Congresso internazionale di Londra," *RDC* 2 (1872): 403–404.

13.   The contract system was widely used in American and European penitentiaries. See, for example, Glen A. Gildemeister, *Prison Labor and Conract Competition with Free Workers in Industrializing America, 1840–1890* (New York: Garland Publishing, Inc., 1987).

14.   *Transactions*, 149–150.

15.   "Congresso internazionale di Londra," 405–406.

16.   See Di Rudinì's report on the proposed budget for the Italian prison administration in 1873, for example, in "Atti parlamentari," *RDC* 3 (1873): 494–495.

17. "Atti parlamentari: Discussione sopra una petizione di fabbricanti di generi di calzoleria della città di Alessandria," *RDC* 4 (1874): 98–103.

18. "Atti parlamentari: Discussione 18 febbraio 1875," *RDC* 5 (1875): 92.

19. The collapse of the parliamentary majority prevented the implementation of even harsher public security legislation after 1875. For more information on the security policies and philosophy of the *Destra*, see Richard Bach Jensen, "Liberty and Order: The Theory and Practice of Italian Public Security Policy," (Ph.D. diss., University of Minn., 1983).

20. Jensen, "Liberty and Order," 85.

21. See the royal decree, dated 19 January 1878, in *Bulletino ufficiale della Direzione generale delle carceri* (Rome) 8, no. 1–2 (1878): 25–26.

22. Davis, *Conflict and Control*, 213–214.

23. "Atti parlamentari," *RDC* 2 (1872): 587–588.

24. "Atti parlamentari," *RDC* 5 (1875): 21. It should also be noted that deputies on the Left also complained that the policy of holding the accused without trial was illiberal and violated individual rights. See the various protests in "Atti parlamentari," *RDC* 2 (1872): 43, 587–88, 591–92.

25. Davis, *Conflict and Control*, 214. The policy of preventive detention was consistently criticized until changes were made in 1913. In 1886, for example, the renowned Jesse White Mario wrote in *The Nation* about the cost and unfairness of preventive detention:

> A law which weighs most hardly upon the poorer classes, and which was pointed out as a crying abuse . . . is the law that allows a stupid or revengeful policeman or praetor or magistrate . . . to cast a man, woman, or child in prison, to keep him there weeks, months, and years without ever bringing him to trial, very often without him knowing what he is accused of. There are at the present moment . . . 20,000 untried prisoners in the various parts of Italy. . . . Now apart from the injury and injustice done to these people and their families, it should be noted that each individual costs the state a franc per day, without, of course, calculating the expense of prisons, jailers. . . . So another seven million goes in wasteful cruelty.

For more on her opinions of Italy's crime problem, see Jesse White Mario, "Misery, Discontent, and Agitation in Italy," *The Nation*, no. 1078 (25 February 1886): 167.

26. For the presentation of the new regulations to Parliament, see "Riordinamento del personale di custodia delle carceri e luoghi di pena," *RDC* 3 (1873): 101–147.

27. This school opened in 1875 in Rome. Giuseppe Boschi, the former Director General, argued that it was an unnecessary expense and advocated on-the-job training for new guards. See "Giudizi e osservazioni sull'opera *La riforma penitenziaria in Italia*," *RDC* 9 (1879): 647.

28. For the discussion of the various articles, see "Atti parlamentari: Discussione dello schema di legge per il riordinamento del personale di custodia delle carceri," *RDC* 3 (1873): 171–193, especially 174–178. The question of security was certainly of great concern, as inmates continued to escape from Italy's prisons at an abnormally high rate. In 1873, for example, four violent criminals (including one sentenced to death for murder) fled from a custodial prison in the South. This episode prompted *The Times* of London to declare that Italy had a severe security problem. For more on this incident, as well as the director general's rebuttal, see "Le carceri in Italia," *RDC* 3 (1873): 348–350 and 394–395.

29. "Atti parlamentari: Stato di prima previsione della spesa del Ministero dell'Interno," *RDC* 5 (1875): 499.

30. "Atti parlamentari: Sulla liberazione condizionale dei condannati," *RDC* 6 (1876): 311–313.

31. Debates continue as to how much the Italian Left really differed from the Italian Right, especially given the *trasformismo* that characterized Italian politics during the premiership of Agostino Depretis. There is no doubt, however, that the Left achieved several notable reforms, including the Coppino Law and the electoral law of 1882. For more information, see Seton-Watson, 41–97; Mack Smith, *Italy*, 102–140; Candeloro, *Storia*, 102–113; and G. Carocci, *Agostino Depretis e la politica interna italiana dal 1876 al 1887* (Turin: Einaudi, 1956).

32. "Atti parlamentari: Discussione 13 febbraio 1879," *RDC* 9 (1879): 77.

33. Ibid., 78.

34. As is well known, Crispi was forced to resign his post because of a scandal in which he was accused of bigamy.

35. For a list of the goals, see Italy. Ministero dell'Interno. Direzione generale delle carceri, *Relazione del Direttore generale e degli ispettori delle carceri per gli anni 1878–1883* (Rome: Tip. delle Mantellate, 1884), 11–13.

36. For the decree naming the commission, see *Bulletino ufficiale della Direzione generale delle carceri* (Rome) 9, no. 1–2 (1879): 3. For more information on the two sessions of the committee, see "Atti parlamentari," *RDC* 10 (1880): 254–255.

37. It should be noted that the office of director general of the prisons was temporarily abolished (February 1878–September 1879) in an unsuccessful effort to save money by decentralizing the prison administration. For the decree reestablishing the office, see *Bulletino ufficiale della Direzione generale delle carceri* 9, no. 10 (1879): 129–130.

38. Beltrani-Scalia, *La riforma penitenziaria*, 210–218.

39. The conditions of the custodial prisons continued to offend numerous parliamentary deputies. Calls for the realization of the 1864 law had been repeatedly slowed, however, because of lack of money. For a sampling of parliamentary opinion, see "Atti parlamentari," *RDC* 3 (1873): 486–521; "Atti parlamentari," *RDC* 4 (1874): 234–242; and "Atti parlamentari," *RDC* 5 (1875): 69–112.

40. Beltrani-Scalia, *La riforma penitenziaria*, 224–233.
41. Prisoners convicted of either brigandage or blackmail, and recidivists in homicide or theft, would not be permitted to move on to the second stage. Ibid., 259.
42. Ibid., 258–61. Again, prisoners convicted of violent crimes like murder remained ineligible for parole.
43. Primarily because of the first stage of cellular isolation. See ibid., 270.
44. Ibid., 273.
45. Ibid., 312. Some ten thousand of the twenty-nine thousand inmates in the penitentiaries and *bagni* were idle in 1875, for example.
46. Ibid., 312–313.
47. Ibid., 315–318. It should be noted that Italy also permitted some of the prisoners with good conduct records to work in the agricultural colonies on the islands of Pianosa, Gorgona, and Capraia. No *forzati* from the *bagni penali* were allowed there, however.
48. Ibid., 337–343.
49. Ibid., 274–285.
50. "Relazione sul regolamento relativo agl'Ispettori di Circolo," *Bulletino ufficiale del Direzione generale delle carceri* 11, no. 4 (1881): 87–95.
51. For a copy of the circular detailing the duties of the district inspectors, see Ministero dell'Interno *Relazione*, 46–59.
52. Ibid., 207–217.
53. "Atti parlamentari," *RDC* 10 (1880): 560.
54. Ibid., 570.
55. The mortality rate had, in fact, reached its highest levels in the summer of 1883, with 5.6 per 100 deaths compared to 1.9 per 100 deaths in 1882. For more information, see Ministero dell'Interno, *Relazione*, 213.
56. "Atti parlamentari," *RDC* 14 (1883): 40–75.
57. These articles are reprinted in "Il lavoro dei condannati all'aperto," *RDC* 10 (1880): 387–410. Carpi had written a book in favor of transportation in 1874. See Martino Beltrani-Scalia's critique of it in "Colonie e deportazione," *RDC* 4 (1874): 403–468.
58. Ibid., 393–394. Beltrani-Scalia also wrote a spirited defense of the colony, "Il lavoro dei condannati all'aperto—L'esperimento alle Tre Fontane e la questione dell'agro romano," in which he listed six reasons why penal agricultural colonies were beneficial to Italy:

1. Prisoners will be employed in the same type of work in prison that they were when free.
2. Prisoners will be able to work while in prison, thus enjoying its moralizing effects, yet will remain skilled in the type of work they practiced before their imprisonment.
3. It will save the State the cost of converting the prisons into industrial workshops.

4.   It will end the possibility of overproduction of certain industrial products in the penitentiaries.

5.   It will eliminate competition between free and prison labor.

6.   It will permit the closure of several underused penitentiaries, thereby saving the state money.

For more of Beltrani-Scalia's views, see this article in *RDC* 10 (1880): 177–213, especially 185.

59.   Aristide Bernabo-Silorata, "L'influenza del lavoro nelle carceri sul libero esercizio dei mestieri in Germania ed in Italia," *RDC* 11 (1881): 73–88, especially 85–86.

60.   For a detailed list of the various ways in which prisoners were employed outside of the *bagni* and the penitentiaries, see "Atti parlamentari," *RDC* 4 (1874): 205. It should also be noted that free workers continued to protest that prison labor was unfair competition. See, for example, the extensive discussion over the use of a prison-operated printing press to publish government works in "Atti parlamentari," *RDC* 14 (1884): 208–210; and Ministero dell'Interno, *Relazione*.

61.   See the circular from Depretis to the Prefects of Italy, dated 28 January 1884, N. 3611–8–1–A, in *Bulletino ufficiale della Direzione generale delle carceri* (Rome) 14, no. 1–2 (1884): 9–11.

62.   "Regolamento per le colonie penali agricole," *Bulletino ufficiale della Direzione generale delle carceri* (Rome) 17, no. 1–2 (1887): 5–14.

63.   Beltrani-Scalia had long stressed the importance of accurate statistics on Italy's prison system. At the First International Prison Congress in 1872, he had proposed a comparative statistical study of all European prisons. See *Transactions*, 487.

64.   "Atti parlamentari," *RDC* 14 (1884): 272.

65.   "Atti parlamentari: Discussione 21 giugno 1878," *RDC* 8 (1878): 242–243.

66.   Archivio Centrale dello Stato (hereafter ACS). Ministero dell'Interno. Gabinetto. Rapporti dei Prefetti (1882–1894), Busta 6, Fascicolo 14, "Relazione sullo spirito pubblico e sull'andamento dei servizi amministrativi nella Provincia di Caltanissetta durante II semestre del 1883."

67.   Ministero dell'Interno. *Relazione*, 250–254.

68.   ACS.   Ministero dell'Interno. Direzione generale delle carceri e dei riformatori, Busta 113.

69.   Ibid., Busta 4.

70.   "La riforma carceraria in Italia," *RDC* 17 (1887): 433.

5

The Emergence of the Positive School
of Criminology

The fundamental purpose of Italy's prison system came under close scrutiny after the emergence of the positive school of criminology in the late nineteenth century. The ideas of Cesare Lombroso and his followers challenged prevailing views on crime and punishment, particularly the classical and neoclassical school's longstanding belief that people choose a life of crime of their own free will and that criminals can be rehabilitated through the institution of the prison. The criminal anthropologists argued instead that many criminals were born criminals, not made. The purpose of punishment was not rehabilitation but rather the removal of these dangerous individuals from the rest of honest society. These new and potentially dangerous ideas attracted an extensive but not unanimous following among Italy's lawyers, prison officials, and scientists. The positive school achieved only limited practical reforms in Italy's criminal justice system during its "golden age," the 1870s and 1880s, however. Just the same, criminal anthropology would remain influential and play a role in the reshaping of the Italian prison system during and after the 1890s.

The founder of the new school, Cesare Lombroso, was born in Verona in 1836 to modestly wealthy parents of Jewish heritage. After a decline in the fortunes of his family, Cesare lived temporarily with his maternal grandfather, Davide Levi. The precocious child studied Latin and Greek and also followed closely the political currents of the Risorgimento. He then went on to study at several schools in Verona, and after 1851 pursued private work with the medical doctor Paolo Marzolo (1810–1868). Inspired by his new teacher, Lombroso decided upon his career and earned his degree in medicine from the University of Pavia in 1858.[1]

After graduation, Lombroso volunteered for duty in the medical corps of the Piedmontese army. In the 1860s, after the national unification, he joined the Army in Calabria to help battle the widespread brigandage in the *Mezzogiorno*. He used this opportunity to perform extensive anthropometric work, measuring the bodies of some three thousand soldiers in an effort to determine the racial characteristics of Italians.[2] He later noted that this effort first convinced him that criminals were a breed apart from normal men:

> The idea first came to me in 1864, when, as an army doctor, I
> beguiled my ample leisure time with a series of studies of the
> Italian soldier. From the very beginning, I was struck by a
> characteristic that distinguished the honest soldier from his
> vicious comrade: the extent to which the latter was tattooed and
> the indecency of the designs that covered his body.[3]

After this brief but productive stint in the army, Lombroso worked at several insane asylums in northern Italy. He continued his study of the anatomical features of the criminal and the criminal insane to determine what, if any, biological features separated the normal man from the criminal and insane man. It was while this question of criminal responsibility filled his mind that he performed an autopsy of the Italian brigand, Vilella. Upon opening the skull, he discovered a depression that he called the median occipital fossa, a characteristic that he knew to be found in lower species of animals.[4] He later wrote that this discovery provided the answer to the question of criminal responsibility:

> This was not merely an idea, but a flash of inspiration. At the
> sight of that skull, I seemed to see all of a sudden, lighted up as
> a vast plain under a flaming sky, the problem of the nature of the
> criminal—an atavistic being who reproduces in his person the
> ferocious instincts of primitive humanity and the inferior animals.
> Thus were explained anatomically the enormous jaws, the high
> cheek bones, prominent superciliary arches, solitary lines in the
> palms, extreme size of the orbits, handle-shaped ears found in
> criminals, savages, and apes, insensibility to pain, extremely
> acute eyesight, tattooing, excessive idleness, love of orgies, and
> the irresponsible craving of evil for its own sake, the desire not
> only to extinguish life in the victim, but to mutilate the corpse,
> tear its flesh and drink its blood.[5]

In other words, Lombroso had formulated his now famous theory that criminals are identifiable by a series of atavistic physical anomalies. These features were present in human ancestors but not in modern men. These atavistic individuals, "throwbacks" to an earlier age of human development, were incapable of thinking at an advanced level, as they had not evolved to that point, and thus necessarily behaved in a manner that modern society deemed criminal.[6]

Lombroso spent the remainder of his life elaborating and developing his idea that criminals are "savages among us." In the wake of sustained criticism from other scientists and legal theorists, he eventually expanded his biological conception of crime to include B. A. Morel's theory of degeneration.[7] He also argued that all born criminals were affected with some level of epilepsy.[8] He further developed the idea that about 50 percent of all criminals were "criminaloids," or people whose innate criminal tendencies were brought out only by social, economic, or climatic factors.[9]

The theory of atavism attracted little attention when Lombroso first presented it in the early 1870s to the Royal Lombardian Institute of Science and Letters. But his key work, *L'Uomo delinquente (Criminal Man)*, published in 1876, found an audience among Italy's scientists and criminologists.[10] With the publication of the second edition of the same work in 1878, in which he expanded the statistical evidence for his conclusions about criminal man, Lombroso won the international fame that he would enjoy for the rest of his life. By 1880, he and his followers had established a journal, the *Archivio di psichiatria, scienze penali, ed antropologia criminale*, that provided the emerging school of criminal anthropology with a forum for its research and conclusions.[11]

One of the most frequent contributors to the new journal over the next few decades was Lombroso's key disciple, Enrico Ferri. Born in Mantua in 1856, the son of a petty bourgeois shopkeeper, Ferri eventually found the intellectual discipline to excel under the tutelage of Roberto Ardigò at the Liceo Virgilio in Mantua. Attracted to the question of criminal responsibility as a student at the University of Bologna, he won notoriety when he challenged the prevailing classical and neoclassical belief that people engage in criminal behavior of their own free will. He then continued his studies at the University of Pisa, again winning recognition for his dissertation on the absence of free will in criminal behavior.[12]

Given his early intellectual leanings, it is not surprising that Ferri gravitated toward Lombroso and his teachings. After a year abroad in France, where he pursued studies on French criminality in the nineteenth century, Ferri went to the University of Turin to study with Lombroso[13] and establish a stronger empirical basis for his theories on criminality. Here he learned more about the biological bases of criminal behavior and also began to explore the social causes of crime.[14]

Ferri provided criminal anthropology with a dynamic and persuasive public voice over the next few decades. A gifted teacher and speaker, he used his lectures at many Italian universities to underline the differences between the positive school and the classical school of criminology. More than anyone else, he defined and established the positive school of criminology as a scientific and empirical approach to crime more suited to the modern age than the metaphysics of the classicists.[15] Even more importantly, he won a seat in the Chamber of Deputies in the 1880s as a deputy from Mantua. Through this office and through his activities as a prominent member of the Italian Socialist party, he sought to effect reform in Italy's criminal justice system along positivist lines.[16]

Ferri also helped Lombroso organize a viable classification system of criminal types. Lombroso had never claimed that all people who commit crimes were biologically determined to a life of crime, but it was Ferri who devised a scientific classification system of criminals that encompassed both hereditary and non-biological social causes of crime. This scheme comprised five classes of delinquents that included the born criminal, the insane criminal, the habitual criminal, the occasional criminal, and the passional criminal. The first group, the born criminals, covered the atavistic beings described by Lombroso that were hereditarily predisposed to crime. The criminal insane, the second category, were those who committed crimes because they suffered from some type of mental illness. The third class, the occasional criminals, were not hereditarily predisposed to crime but rather broke the law because of their socioeconomic conditions. The habitual delinquents, the fourth group, usually began as occasional criminals, but "acquired the habit of crime mainly through the ineffective measures employed by society for the prevention and repression of crime." The last type of offender, the passional criminal, usually committed violent crimes after his passions were aroused; he was otherwise a completely normal person. Although Ferri recognized that his scheme was arbitrary and did not cover every type of criminal, he argued that a classification system was required for a scientific approach to the treatment of criminals.[17]

The positive school's new definitions of the origins of criminal behavior did not call into question the concept of punishment but certainly demanded a new conceptualization of the purpose of punishment. Lombroso and his followers generally argued that punishment must be designed to fit the criminal, not the crime he had committed. As long as a criminal could be considered a threat to society, he should be segregated from the rest of honest society.

Lombroso himself expressed little confidence in the reformative possibilities of the prison. He argued that the prison was rather a world unto itself, populated by a breed of persons who spoke their own distinctive language. After an extensive study of the songs, graffiti, and tattoos of prisoners in two cellular prisons in northern Italy, Lombroso concluded that the rule of silence was a sham and that prisoners continued to communicate with each other and form criminal associations. He offered this work as evidence that cellular prisons did not lead to the rehabilitation of criminals into honest men but simply encouraged them in their criminal activities. He thus urged the Italian government to reconsider its policy of spending thousands of lire on the construction of new penitentiaries.[18]

Lombroso also attacked the idea that inmates could benefit from elementary education while in prison. Contrary to contemporary beliefs that education would prevent prisoners from returning to a life of crime, Lombroso argued just the opposite:

> Elementary education is positively harmful as applied to the ordinary criminal. . . . The introduction of schools into prisons, at once bringing bad men into contact with each other and developing their intelligence, explain, to my mind, the great number of educated recidivists.[19]

The Italian government was thus well advised, in Lombroso's opinion, to refrain from its already limited efforts to establish prison schools.

Given his lack of faith in the reformative possibilities of the cellular prison, it is not surprising that Lombroso advocated several alternative types of punishment. He recommended, for example, that occasional criminals should only pay simple damages to the family of the victim, plus fines if they committed the crime again. So too, Lombroso argued, criminals of passion suffered remorse for their crime and would most likely not commit a similar infraction. Thus, they were not dangerous to society, and they could be fined or exiled from the place where the offense had been committed.[20] Political crimes also called for fines and temporary exile.[21]

Lombroso recommended the use of institutions for the criminal insane, the habitual delinquent, and the born criminal. These types of offenders would be given an indeterminate sentence in a criminal asylum, a prison, or an agricultural colony such as Tre Fontane. There they could engage in fruitful labor in fields or workshops, depending on their aptitude. They would be released only after a panel of "experts" that consisted of criminal anthropologists, physicians, and judges deemed them reformed and no further threat to honest society.[22]

Like Lombroso, Ferri argued that the wide spectrum of criminal types demanded a similarly broad system of punishment. He, too, called for the individualization of punishment in a system of social defense. For most criminals, fines and reparations to the victims would suffice.[23] Those who were sentenced to an institution must be admitted to a new type of penal establishment:

> The common and fundamental character of all different establishments where delinquents for whom reparation in damages is not a sufficient punishment are isolated, must change from prisons, or places of torture and slavery, into establishments of physical and moral treatment, with discipline suited to the diverse forms of criminal tendency, similar to hospitals, special clinics, and insane asylums.[24]

Ferri, however, did not want to be seen as "soft" on criminals; he thus stressed that the inmates in these institutions should pay for their room and board by working in agricultural pursuits or industrial workshops. Indeed, he suggested that some of these inmates should be used to reclaim malaria-infested lands, arguing that "it is much better to immolate criminals than honest farmers."[25]

Both Ferri and Lombroso were philosophically unopposed to the death penalty. Ferri held, for example, that society had the right to practice "artificial selection" and eliminate the socially unfit in the same way that nature used the process of natural selection. Unlike Lombroso, however, he maintained that capital punishment served no useful purpose in modern society because it was used so sparingly. Unless society was willing to execute all of its undesirables, the death penalty might as well be abolished.[26]

Ferri also asserted that a system of social defense required a series of preventive measures to supplement and perhaps eventually supplant repressive means of punishment. He proposed a series of "penal substitutes" that would alter or eliminate the social and economic conditions that promoted criminal activities. So, for example, he maintained that the introduction of free trade would help eradicate property crimes. A reduction of the import taxes would result in a corresponding decline in smuggling. Freedom of speech would help eliminate political crimes because the masses would respect the ruling authorities. Overall, Ferri believed that preventive measures like these could eliminate nine-tenths of all crimes.[27]

These new ideas on punishment, as well as the positive school's general conception of the origins of crime, attracted a wide following in Italy and the rest of Europe during the 1880s. The publication of successive editions of *L'uomo delinquente* continued to win international praise and admiration. Many Italian legal theorists and politicians anticipated that Lombroso's ideas would provide the ideological basis of the new penal code. In Argentina, plans were made to do just that.[28]

This tremendous popularity may be explained at a variety of levels. First, these theories appealed to the positivistic and scientific spirit of the age. The clear relationship between Lombroso's concept of atavism and evolutionary theory tied the positive school directly to Charles Darwin and the key scientific debate of the late nineteenth century.[29] Buttressing their theories with masses of statistics, the criminal anthropologists seemed to offer a scientific explanation of criminal behavior. Ferri promised that reform in the prison system and penal laws along positivistic lines could eliminate crime. Such optimism injected a new sense of intellectual excitement into the prosaic era of the *postrisorgimento*.[30]

The positive school also explained to many the key legal question of the day, the question of criminal responsibility. It must be remembered that Lombroso addressed that very problem when he formulated his theory of atavism. His daughter and biographer, Gina Lombroso-Ferrero, later maintained that he offered "the right idea at the right time," as many legal theorists were disillusioned with the classical belief that people committed crimes of their own free will.[31]

Besides responding to current legal questions, Lombroso and the criminal anthropologists also spoke to the social and political problems confronting late-nineteenth-century Italy. The young country had earned a reputation for a "sad primacy" in crime, and criminal statistics pointed to a marked increase in violent crimes such as murder.[32] Indeed, Ferri saw Italy's crime rate as a stimulus to the development of criminal anthropology:

> The positive school of criminology, then, was born in our own Italy through the singular attraction of the Italian mind towards the study of criminology; and its birth is also due to the peculiar condition of our country with its great and strange contrast between the theoretical doctrines and the painful fact of an ever-increasing criminality.[33]

As Daniel Pick has argued, the criminal anthropologists appeared to offer a scientific formula to identify and help eliminate the undesirable elements from the Italian body politic. They also offered comforting evidence that once those criminal elements so dominant in southern Italy were eliminated, the crime rate would diminish and the country would prosper.[34]

Despite this fanfare, however, the positive school could claim few practical reforms during the 1880s. The one development that proved promising was the establishment, on an experimental basis, of an asylum for mentally ill criminals (*manicomio criminale*). As early as 1872, Lombroso had called for the creation of such institutions to house both those who had committed a crime and then were found to be mentally ill, and those who went insane while they were in prison. He argued that the mentally ill who were deemed incorrigible and "habitually dangerous" should be committed for life. They should not live a life of ease, however, but should be compelled to work, with occasional leisure time for games like billiards. Inmates found to be temporarily insane would be eligible for release after a few years but would remain subject to monthly surveillance by medical personnel.[35]

The desire to establish asylums for the criminal insane was not unique to the positive school, however. Numerous psychiatrists, prison officials, and classical legal theorists shared this enthusiasm for the creation of asylums for the criminal insane. But they called for such institutions primarily because mentally ill prisoners caused extreme disorder in regular penitentiaries, not because they saw the criminal insane as a unique type of offender. By 1876, a section of the penitentiary at Aversa had been set aside for mentally ill prisoners from across Italy.[36] In 1881 and again in 1884, the minister of the interior, Agostino Depretis, presented a proposal to the Chamber of Deputies to authorize and define asylums for insane criminals.[37]

While awaiting legislative approval, the prison administration organized an asylum for the criminal insane at the Villa Medicea dell'Ambrogiana in Florence. By 1888, this establishment housed one hundred inmates from penitentiaries and custodial prisons across Italy. The prison administration fully expected that this experimental institution would win legislative approval and that several more such asylums would be constructed after the completion of the new penal code.[38]

The limited practical success of the positive school of criminology in the 1880s resulted from the extensive criticism that emerged on several fronts during that decade. Many traditional legal theorists, for example, rejected most of the conclusions of the positive school of criminology. Schooled in the Beccaria tradition, this "classical" or "neoclassical" school of criminology judged the criminal's offense rather than the criminal himself. Punishment, they argued, must be based on the perceived seriousness of the crime and not on the biological, mental, or moral state of the offender. They revised the hedonistic calculus of the classical school, however, to allow some degree of individual responsibility for a crime. They advocated the use of the penitentiary as a humane punishment and effective deterrent to crime. And, of course, they completely opposed the death penalty as useless in modern society.[39]

But many members of the classical school betrayed a certain ambivalence to the conclusions of the classical school, particularly on the question of criminal responsibility. Several legal theorists, as noted above, supported the institution of asylums for the criminal insane, even though these institutions violated the classical conception of criminal responsibility. And some of the judges and lawyers trained along classical lines, most notably Baron Raffaele Garofalo,[40] accepted completely the positions of the positive school.

Luigi Lucchini (1847–1929), a law professor at the University of Bologna, revealed this ambivalence in his polemic against the "new school" of criminology, *I semplicisti del diritto penale* (1886). Lucchini did not try to attack criminal anthropology from a purely "classical" point of view. Indeed, he considered himself something of a positivist who based his legal opinions on empirical evidence rather than metaphysical speculations on human free will. He rather tried to show that Lombroso and his followers were not positivists at all but rather pseudoscientists who presented unscientific evidence and arbitrary conclusions as truth. In other words, he focused on the weaknesses in Lombroso's methodology rather than on the problems with Lombroso's conclusions.[41]

Enrico Ferri noted Lucchini's irresolute stance on the question of criminal responsibility in a spirited rebuttal of *I semplicisti del diritto penale*. He also argued that Lucchini had violated the cardinal rule of scientific work by misrepresenting the ideas of the positive school. Ferri pointed out, for example, that Lucchini's claim that the positive school called for the execution of all insane criminals proved that he had misunderstood Garofalo's concept of psychic anomalies. He also defended the use of the death penalty against Lucchini's criticism of the idea of artificial selection. And he could not resist ridiculing Lucchini's suggestion that inmates be permitted some sexual relations during their prison terms, noting that while "our society does not provide the daily bread and legitimate love to thousands of poor *honest* folk . . . you would provide the murderers and rapists in the *bagni penali* with sexual intercourse at the expense of the state."[42]

The Italian prison administration displayed a similarly mixed position on the ideas of the positive school of criminology. Martino Beltrani-Scalia, the best known official in the prison bureaucracy, agreed with Lombroso and Ferri on the need for preventive measures against crime. He also supported the creation of the asylums for the criminally insane. But not surprisingly, he could not accept Lombroso's argument that prisons only bred more crime. Questioning Lombroso's use of statistics on recidivists in Italy, Beltrani-Scalia maintained that the prison could and did deter future crime. He argued that the statistics on recidivism would only have meaning after a comprehensive reform of Italy's prisons had taken place. The institution of the prison should be considered an ineffective deterrent to crime only if the Italian crime and recidivism rate remained inordinately high after such a comprehensive reform.[43]

The Italian socialist, Filippo Turati, also offered a number of perceptive criticisms of the positive school of criminology. His most sustained and important attack on the inconsistencies and the conclusions of the works of the positivists was an essay, *Il delitto e la questione sociale* (*Crime and the Social Question*), first published in 1882. Turati objected to the positive school on two grounds. First, he clearly believed that the social and economic conditions characteristic of capitalist and industrial society, and not biology, caused all criminal behavior. In other words, differences in the social and economic circumstances of the social classes in industrial society explained Italy's continuing crime problem. Italy required a fundamental "social transformation" if it hoped to deal with its persistent crime problem. Second, Turati questioned the positive school's methodology and use of statistics. He demonstrated, for example, that it was quite possible to interpret the growth in alcohol consumption in France as a result of social rather than biological factors.[44]

The Roman Catholic Church also proved an unflinching opponent of the ideas of the positive school. Above all, the church objected to the criminal anthropologists' rejection of the moral responsibility of the criminal. Edoardo Agostino Gemelli (1878–1959), an Italian psychologist who was also a Catholic priest, clarified the church's position in several works written after the death of Lombroso. He noted, for example, that the positive school viewed the world as a machine and denied the role of spiritual forces and human free will. Like many of Lombroso's critics, Father Gemelli also questioned the positive school's methodology, calling it anecdotal and unscientific. He argued that the best way to combat crime would be to improve social and economic conditions that promoted criminal behavior, and "above all, to reestablish and intensify religious beliefs."[45]

The Radical parliamentary deputy, Napoleone Colajanni (1847–1921), was also an impassioned critic of the positive school of criminology. Born in Sicily, Colajanni staunchly defended the *Mezzogiorno* in the Chamber of Deputies. He considered the ideas of the positive school to be racist, particularly Lombroso's implication that southern Italy was populated with an inferior breed of human beings. In one of his numerous attacks, Colajanni asserted that because he was from Sicily, Lombroso and the Italian criminal anthropologists refused to take him and his work seriously.[46]

But the least-forgiving critics that Lombroso and the Italian positive school of criminology faced were, ironically, French criminal anthropologists. At the First International Congress of Criminal Anthropology, held in Rome in 1885, the French delegates surprised everyone by questioning the existence of the born criminal. Alexander Lacassagne, a doctor of legal medicine, challenged in particular the hereditary concept of crime and presented the theory that social conditions were fundamental in the development of crime. Echoing Louis Pasteur's recent discoveries, he noted that "the social milieu is the mother of criminality; the microbe is the criminal, an element that gains significance only at the moment it finds the broth that makes it ferment."[47]

Undaunted by these criticisms, the Italian school held firm to its belief in the existence of the born criminal. Ferri, Garofalo, and others asserted, in fact, that classical conceptions of free will and criminal responsibility were on the brink of disappearing. They believed that no criticism of their methods could refute their claims to scientific truth about the nature of criminal man. The Congress closed with many foreign criminal anthropologists still expressing support for the Italian school of criminal anthropology.[48]

The developing rift between the Italian and French criminal anthropologists intensified at the Second International Congress of Criminal Anthropology, held in Paris in 1889. The French delegation, represented by Paul Topinard, Leone Manouvrier, Gabriel Tarde, and Lacassagne, again stressed the primacy of social rather than hereditary factors in the development of the criminal. Much to Lombroso's chagrin, Manouvrier, an anthropologist from Paris' Ecole d'anthropologie, characterized the work of Italy's criminal anthropologists as a pseudoscience in the vein of Franz Gall's phrenology. He then pointed out one of

Lombroso's chief methodological failings—the lack of a control group of "honest" men to compare with criminal men. Manouvrier further declared that Enrico Ferri's typology of criminals, which took into account social causes of crime, was similarly unscientific and arbitrary.[49]

In the wake of this and other attacks, the Italian criminal anthropologists proposed that an impartial committee be created to examine one hundred criminals and one hundred honest men. Lombroso and the other Italian delegates presumed that the results of this study would prove the existence of the born criminal and silence the French criticism of their research methods. But the study was never undertaken, apparently because the appointed commission deemed it unnecessary. Lombroso and his supporters then broke away completely from the French school of criminal anthropology and decided to boycott the next international congress, held in Brussels in 1892. In the ensuing years, the French would continue their assault against the Italian position at other international congresses and in their journal, the *Archives d'anthropologie criminelle.*[50]

During the next few decades, Lombroso and his followers witnessed a slow decline in the international reputation of the Italian school of criminal anthropology. But their theories paved the way for some fundamental changes in the study and treatment of the criminal. First, their demand for a clinical and scientific investigation of the individual criminal became standard procedure for many criminologists. Second, their call for the use of preventive measures and indeterminate sentencing in a system of social defense influenced the reform of numerous penal systems, including that of the United States. Finally, it should be remembered that if nothing else, the Italian school's ideas prompted an extensive reexamination and discussion of criminal justice systems everywhere.[51]

In Italy, the positive school of criminology remained influential even beyond Lombroso's death in 1909. Criminal anthropologists won professorial chairs at Italian universities that were formerly the haven of the classical school.[52] Members of the positive school of criminology also engaged in an unrelenting campaign to change Italy's criminal justice system along positivist lines. Even though they would only partially influence the new penal code in the late 1880s, they would successfully influence reforms, particularly in Italy's penal and police systems in the 1890s and early 1900s.

Notes

1.   Lombroso has been the subject of several biographies since his death in 1909. His daughter and disciple, Gina Lombroso-Ferrero, penned a detailed, if uncritical, study in 1914 entitled *Cesare Lombroso: storia della vita e delle opere*, 2nd ed. (Bologna: Nicola Zanichelli, 1921). Another contemporary and student of Lombroso, the German doctor Hans Kurella, also wrote a comprehensive work on Lombroso, *Cesare Lombroso: A Modern Man of Science*, trans. M. Eden Paul (New York: Rebman Company, 1910).

In recent times, the two most notable biographies include Luigi Bulferetti's lengthy study, *Cesare Lombroso* (Turin: UTET, 1975) and Renzo Villa, *Il deviante e i suoi segni* (Milan: Franco Angeli, 1985). For a good brief overview of Lombroso's career, see Marvin E. Wolfgang, "Cesare Lombroso," in Hermann Mannheim, ed., *Pioneers in Criminology*, 2nd ed. (Montclair, N. J.: Patterson Smith, 1972), 232–291.

2.   On Lombroso's military career, see Lombroso-Ferrero, *Criminal Man*, 67–93; and Bulferetti, *Cesare Lombroso*, 93–120.

3.   Quoted in Wolfgang, "Cesare Lombroso," 247.

4.   On Lombroso's early work in the asylums and prisons of northern Italy, see Lombroso-Ferrero, *Criminal Man*, 101–103 and 129–143. It should also be noted that Lombroso devoted much of his energy during these years exploring the causes of pellagra. He eventually concluded that the disease resulted from corn that had been stored improperly. For the hostile reception of this theory by the Italian government and Lombard landowners, see Kurella, *Cesare Lombroso: A Modern Man of Science*, 149–156; and Bulferetti, *Cesare Lombroso*, 213–230.

5.   This famous quote can be found in almost any study of Lombroso. Here it is taken from Daniel Pick, *Faces of Degeneration* (Cambridge: Cambridge University Press, 1989), 122.

6.   Lombroso's theory of atavism was, predictably, the most controversial aspect of his work. The natural historian, Stephen Jay Gould, has pointed out Lombroso's key mistake in formulating this theory:

> Lombroso's anatomical stigmata were, for the most part, neither pathologies nor discontinuous variations, but extreme values on a normal curve that approach average measures for the same trait in great apes. In modern terms, this is the fundamental source of Lombroso's error. Arm length varies among humans, and some people must have longer arms than others. The average chimp has a longer arm than the average human, but this doesn't mean that a relatively long-armed human is genetically similar to apes. Normal variation within a population is a different biological phenomenon from differences in average values *between* populations. . . . A true atavism is a discontinuous, genetically based, ancestral trait.

For Gould's critical review of Lombroso's conclusions, see his *The Mismeasure of Man* (New York: W. W. Norton, 1981), 122–145.

7.   For more information on Lombroso's revisions along these lines, see Bulferetti, *Cesare Lombroso*. 280–300, and Villa, *Il deviante*, 163–195. On Morel, see Pick, *Faces of Degeneration*, 44–59.

8.   The case of an Italian soldier, Misdea, who suddenly killed eight of his comrades, convinced Lombroso of the epileptic nature of born criminals. See Cesare Lombroso and S. Bianchi, "Misdea," *Archivio di psichiatria, scienze penali, ed antropologia criminale* (Turin) 5 (1884): 382–402, especially 394–401.

9.   Lombroso presented the idea of criminaloids in later editions of *L'Uomo delinquente*. See, for example, *Crime: Its Causes and Remedies*, trans. Henry P. Horton (Boston: Little, Brown, and Co., 1912), especially part I. This work is the English translation of a later French version of *L'uomo delinquente*.

10.   See the favorable review of this edition in "Bibliografia," *RDC* 6 (1876): 472–477. For a brief excerpt from the first edition of *L'Uomo delinquente*, consult Sawyer F. Sylvester, Jr., ed., *The Heritage of Modern Criminology* (Cambridge, Mass.: Schenkman Publishing Company, 1972), 67–78.

11.   Lombroso's daughter contended that this journal gave Lombroso his greatest happiness. See Lombroso-Ferrero, *Cesare Lombroso*, 207–208, 220–223.

12.   Enrico Ferri still awaits his biographer. For a good brief study of his life and work, however, consult Thorsten Sellin, "Enrico Ferri," in Hermann Mannheim, *Pioneers in Criminology*, 361–384. See also the entry on Ferri in Frank J. Coppa, ed., *Dictionary of Modern Italian History* (Westport, Conn.: Greenwood Press, 1985), 156–157. For Ferri's controversial conclusions on the role of free will in human behavior, see his *La teoria dell'imputabilita e la negazione del libero arbitrio* (Florence, 1878).

13.   In 1876, Lombroso was named Professor of Legal Medicine at the University of Turin.

14.   Sellin, "Enrico Ferri," 362–68; and Lombroso-Ferrero, *Criminal Man*, 214–216.

15.   Ferri calculated that he had given some three thousand university and public lectures during his lifetime. See Sellin, "Enrico Ferri," 364. For a typical set of lectures in which he stressed the differences between the positive and classical schools of criminology, see his *The Positive School of Criminology*, trans. Ernest Untermann (Chicago: Charles H. Kerr and Company, 1913).

16.   By the mid-1890s, Ferri was a prominent leader of the Italian Socialist party's revolutionary wing. He also was the editor of the party's newspaper, *Avanti!,* from 1897–1904. For more information, see A. James Gregor, *Young Mussolini and the Intellectual Origins of Fascism* (Berkeley: University of California Press, 1979), especially 12–21. Ferri's effectiveness as a parliamentary deputy will be discussed in chapters 6, 7, and 8.

17. Ferri formulated this typology in an article for the *Archivio*. Although he continued to refine it in successive editions of his key work, *Criminal Sociology*, he never really deviated from these five basic classes of criminals. See his *Criminal Sociology*, trans. Joseph I. Kelly and John Lisle (Boston: Little, Brown, and Co., 1917), 138–159.

18. See Cesare Lombroso, *I palimsesti del carcere* (Turin: Bocca, 1888), especially 323. In a review of this work for the official journal of the Italian prison administration, a disciple of Lombroso, Scipio Sighele, argued that this book was most useful precisely because it showed that the cost of constructing cellular prisons exceeded their advantages. See "Bibliografia," *RDC* (Rome) 21 (1891): 331–333.

19. Lombroso, *Crime: Its Causes and Remedies*, 114.

20. Ibid., 410–415. See also Lombroso's early work on the means needed for a system of social defense, *Sull'incremento del delitto in Italia e sui mezzi per arrestarlo* (Turin: Bocca, 1879), especially Part II.

21. Lombroso devoted an entire study to political criminals. He urged light and temporary punishment of their infractions, as he did not consider them dangerous. See his *Il delitto politico e le rivoluzioni* (Turin: Bocca, 1890).

22. Lombroso, *Crime*, 386–387, 419–425.

23. Ferri, *Criminal Sociology*, 537–543.

24. Ibid., 518.

25. Ibid., 535.

26. Ibid., 528–531. Clearly, Ferri's argument could easily be distorted to justify exactly what he believed society would be unwilling to do—execute social "undesirables" *en masse*. Indeed, George Mosse argues that the Nazis used the ideas of the positive school, especially Lombroso's definition of the "habitual criminal," to justify the extermination of the Jews. As he says, "the Jews because of their race were regarded as habitual criminals by the Nazis and therefore rightly doomed to destruction." For more information, see George L. Mosse, *Toward the Final Solution: A History of European Racism* (New York: Howard Fertig, 1978), especially 84 and 219–220.

27. Ferri, *Positive School*, 115–124; and Ferri, *Criminal Sociology*, 226, 246–282.

28. In 1890, the Argentine president created a committee to prepare a new penal code that reflected the ideas of the positive school of criminology. Among other thing, the new code, completed in 1891, included reparations to victims of crime. See Lombroso-Ferrero, *Criminal Man*, 285.

29. On the links between Lombroso and evolutionary theory, see Stephen Jay Gould, *Ontogeny and Phylogeny* (Cambridge, Mass.: Belknap, 1977), 120–125; Susanna Barrows, *Distorting Mirrors: Visions of the Crowd in Late Nineteenth-Century France* (New Haven, Conn.: Yale University Press, 1981), especially 125–126; and Giuliano Pancaldi, *Darwin in Italia: Impresa scientifica e frontiere culturali* (Bologna: Mulino, 1983), especially 263–286.

30. Benedetto Croce discussed this "cult of positivist tendencies," as well as the eventual reaction against it, in his *A History of Italy*, trans. Cecilia M. Ady (Oxford: Clarendon Press, 1929), especially 126–143. See also Robert A. Nye, *Crime, Madness, and Politics in Modern France* (Princeton: Princeton Univ. Press, 1984), 100–101.

31. Lombroso-Ferrero, *Criminal Man*, 211.

32. Lombroso detailed the high crime rate in Italy in his, *Sull'incremento*, 1–6. See also, Davis, *Conflict and Control*, 314–316.

33. Ferri, *Positive School of Criminology*, 14–15.

34. Pick, *Faces of Degeneration*, 126–128.

35. Lombroso's early work on asylums for the criminal insane, *Sull'istituzione dei manicomi criminali in Italia* (1872), is discussed in Romano Canosa, *Storia del manicomio in Italia dall'Unità a oggi* (Milan: Feltrinelli, 1979), 136–137. See also Augusto Tamburini, "Dei manicomi criminali e di una lacune nelle odierna legislazione," *RDC* 6 (1876): 440–456. It should be noted that Lombroso argued that the case of Davide Lazzaretti proved the need for these asylums. See his *Sull'incremento*, 105.

36. Beltrani-Scalia, *La riforma penitenziaria*, 342–343.

37. For excerpts from the proposal of 1881, see "Manicomi criminali," *RDC* 11 (1881): 145–153.

38. For a description, including plates, of the *manicomio criminale* in Florence, see Leopoldo Ponticelli and C. Algeri, "Il manicomio criminale dell'Ambrogiana," *RDC* 18 (1888): 3–27.

39. On the nature and origins of the classical school of criminology, see John Lewis Gillin, *Criminology and Penology* (New York: D. Appleton-Century Company, 1935), 216–225; Lewis Yablonsky, *Criminology*, 4th ed. (New York: Harper and Row, 1990), 425–426; and Ferri, *Criminal Sociology*, 1–7.

40. Garofalo (1852–1934) is considered by many as the third key member of Lombroso's school of criminal anthropology. He won renown in his native city of Naples for his work as a lawyer, judge, and university professor. Attracted to Lombroso's ideas while a student, he eventually joined the editorial staff of the *Archivio di psichiatria*.

Like Lombroso and Ferri, Garofalo believed that scientific methods must be used to analyze the origins of crime and the nature of the criminal. He also agreed that the system of punishment needed to be revised to include the death penalty and reparations for victims. He differed from Lombroso, however, because he focused on what he termed "psychic" or "moral" anomalies (not necessarily inherited) rather than physical stigmata. As he saw it, the true criminal was a person whose underdeveloped or absent sense of altruism led him to commit crimes against the "sentiments of pity and probity." Examples of offenses to the "sentiment of pity" included violence to persons, while crimes against the "sentiment of probity" embraced property crimes and embezzlement. For more on Garofalo's views on crime and punishment, see his major work, *Criminology*, trans. Robert Wyness

Millar (Montclair, N. J.: Patterson Smith, 1968), which was first published in 1885. On Garofalo's life, see Francis A. Allen, "Raffaele Garofalo," in Hermann Mannheim, ed., *Pioneers in Criminology*, 317–340.

41. Luigi Lucchini, *I semplicisti del diritto penale* (Turin: UTET, 1886). See also Ugo Spirito, *Storia del diritto penale italiano da Cesare Beccaria ai nostri giorni* (Florence: G. C. Sansoni, 1974), 174–177.

42. Enrico Ferri, "Uno spiritista del diritto penale," chap. in *Studi sulla criminalità* (Turin: Bocca, 1901), 334–338, especially 349. This article was first published in the *Archivio di psichiatria, antropologia criminale, ed scienze penale* 8 (1887).

43. Beltrani-Scalia, *La riforma*, 212–217, 342–343. Several criminal anthropologists acknowledged Beltrani-Scalia's liberal attitude towards their work but called upon him to make a greater effort to collect anthropometric data on prisoners. See the letters from Augusto Tamburini and Giulio Benelli in "L'antropologia nelle carceri," *RDC* 15 (1885): 136–143.

44. Filippo Turati, *Il delitto e la questione sociale*, 3rd ed. (Bologna: Casa Editrice, "La contro-corrente," 1913), especially 64–126; and Davis, 338–341. Turati and Ferri rarely saw eye to eye on political issues as well. Turati supported the reformist wing of the Italian Socialist party that was strongly opposed to Ferri's revolutionary wing of the party.

45. Agostino Gemelli, *Le dottrine moderne della delinquenza*, 3rd ed. (Milan: Società editrice "Vita e pensiero," 1920), 211–212. Daniel Pick argues that Lombroso's Jewish heritage contributed to his opposition to the concept of human free will so fundamental to classical criminology and to Catholic dogma. See Pick, *Faces of Degeneration*, 112.

46. See Dott. Napoleone Colajanni, *Ire e spropositi di Cesare Lombroso* (Catania: Filippo Tropea, 1890), 95–96; and John A. Thayer, *Italy and the Great War: Politics and Culture, 1870–1915* (Madison, Wis.: University of Wisconsin Press, 1964), 31.

47. Quoted in Nye, *Crime, Madness, and Politics*, 104. Robert Nye has thoroughly examined the French and Italian positions at the International Congresses of Criminal Anthropology in his *Crime, Madness, and Politics in Modern France*, especially 103–109. Nye argues that French criminologists refused to adopt a hereditary interpretation of criminal behavior primarily because they realized that French jurists and politicians would never accept a total rejection of the role of free will in the development of criminal behavior. They adopted something of a compromise position as a way to achieve practical reforms in France's criminal justice system. See Nye, *Crime, Madness, and Politics*, 111.

48. Ibid., 104–106; Lombroso-Ferrero, *Criminal Man*, 248–251. See also Robert A. Nye, "Heredity or Milieu: The Foundations of Modern European Criminological Theory," *Isis* 67 (1976): 339–343.

49. Lombroso-Ferrero, *Criminal Man*, 274–281; Nye, *Crime, Madness, and Politics*, 106–108; and Colajanni, *Ire e spropositi*, 98–117.

50. Nye, *Crime, Madness and Politics*, 109–119; Lombroso-Ferrero, *Criminal Man*, 279–281. Ruth Harris has argued that the differences between the French and Italian criminal anthropologists should not be overstated. She stresses, for example, that both schools ultimately promoted "deterministic explanations of criminal behavior." Like the Italians, the French used clinical and scientific methods to study the individual criminal and not just his crime. And they, too, tried to construct classification systems that covered various criminal "types." For more information, see her *Murders and Madness* (Cambridge: Cambridge University Press, 1989), 80–90, especially 88.

51. On the impact of the Italian school, see Gillin, *Criminology and Penology*. 237–238; and Gould, *Mismeasure of Man*, 135–142.

52. Enrico Ferri, for example, replaced Francesco Carrara, the noted classical legal theorist, at the University of Pisa in 1890. See Sellin, "Enrico Ferri," 374.

6

Reform in Italy's Criminal Justice System during the First Premiership of Francesco Crispi, 1887–1891

The first premiership of Francesco Crispi from 1887 to 1891 signaled a new beginning, at least on paper, for Italy's criminal justice system. In spite of the objections of the positive school of criminology, the energetic and authoritarian Crispi engineered the long-awaited unification of the Italian penal code. As minister of the interior, he sponsored key reforms in Italy's public security policy and prison system. He also authorized the director general of the prisons, Martino Beltrani-Scalia, to write the first set of general regulations for Italy's prison system.[1]

Crispi had attempted to initiate prison reform during his brief tenure as minister of the interior in 1878.[2] In May 1887, just a few months before he was named prime minister, Crispi outlined his plans for reform in Italy's criminal justice system during a parliamentary discussion of the budget of the Ministry of the Interior. He was prompted to voice his thoughts on the topic primarily because Deputy Enrico Ferri had taken this opportunity to castigate the Italian prison system and to advance the ideas of the positive school of criminology. Ferri had criticized, for example, the idea that cellular prisons should be the linchpins in any prison system. Instead of locking prisoners up in cells that had no effect on incorrigible habitual criminals and were particularly ill-suited to the Mediterranean temperament, Ferri proposed employing prisoners in public works projects such as land reclamation. Ferri further asserted that the patronage societies (*società di patronato*) that were designed to help inmates upon their release from prison could not stop recidivism. He suggested that it would be more profitable to give the allocated funds to orphanages and attempt to stop crime before it began.[3] Finally, Ferri lambasted the "disparity of treatment" accorded various types of inmates. Typically, he argued, a convicted murderer enjoyed better treatment than an accused person awaiting trial:

> I can truly certify that in the many trips I have made in my
> melancholy visits to penal establishments, I have found that the
> shameful conditions of these institutions follows an inverse
> progression from the *bagno penale* to the police jail. As soon as
> one moves from the major criminals to the minor criminals, from
> the convicted to the accused, one finds that the conditions of the
> buildings deteriorate. . . . But this is not enough: the food
> worsens as well.[4]

Ferri's impassioned pleas to end the "soft" treatment of convicted criminals won the sympathy of the Chamber, and he finished his statements to the cheers and congratulations of many deputies.[5]

In response to Ferri, Giulio Prinetti, who had presented the proposed budget to the Chamber, sounded an optimistic note on the limited achievements of the Italian prison administration. Prinetti noted, for example, that a large part of the budget was directed toward the custodial prisons and not the penitentiaries and *bagni penali*. He further pointed out that the prison administration had made several attempts to use inmates in public works projects such as the construction of the fortifications around Rome. He also argued that the patronage societies that Ferri deemed ineffective were simply in their infancy and would eventually garner the positive results of similar institutions in Great Britain and France. But in the end, even Prinetti was forced to admit that the prison administration faced an uphill battle "as long as Italy is forced to maintain an overflowing prison population."[6]

Similarly unconvinced by Ferri's remarks, the minister of the interior, Crispi, related his ideas on the reforms needed in Italy's criminal justice system. The first requirement, he argued, was the completion of a unified penal code that would provide the guidelines for prison reform and make improvements in the system "much easier." Unlike Ferri, Crispi maintained that the cellular prison should be the basic unit of the prison system. It was required, for example, to prevent the corruption of those awaiting trial. An advocate of the Progressive or Irish system of prison discipline, Crispi envisioned that a prisoner would be isolated in cells for the first part of his sentence, because "it is good that he feels the force of the punishment that was inflicted on him for the crime he had committed."[7] After an initial period of isolation, he would then move onto the other key element of the Irish system, work, "because work is precisely the means of redemption of the convicted."[8] This work would not necessarily be on land reclamation or public works projects, as advocated by Ferri. Continuing his disagreement with Ferri, Crispi asserted that patronage societies must be expanded, not eliminated. As he saw it, these organizations "responded to a great need, because the day when a free prisoner returns to society, he needs protection and aid so that he will become useful to society or, at least, not return to a life of crime."[9]

Crispi called for improved policing methods to complement his proposed reforms in the Italian prison system. He argued that the nature of Italian crime was changing, with a steady increase in property crimes and a corresponding decline in violent crimes.   To stop the rising number of property crimes, Italy needed to change its policing techniques. In particular, Crispi suggested methods that would prevent crimes rather than simply repressing them.[10]

Crispi's discourse to the Chamber proved prophetic. After he was named prime minister in August 1887, he pursued a course of action remarkably similar to the one he had sketched out in the Chamber of Deputies. Ferri and the other criminal anthropologists would have just as difficult a time influencing these reforms, however, as they had trying to sway Crispi's opinions on the proper reform of the Italian penal system in 1887.

According to Crispi's blueprint, Italy required a unified penal code prior to any other reform in the criminal justice system. As we have already seen,[11] disputes over the death penalty had forced the Italian government to accept a tripartite penal code in 1865. The government had made several attempts thereafter to unify the penal code. In 1874 and again in 1877, the Ministry of Justice had presented two projects to the Italian parliament. Both met defeat in the Senate because of continuing opposition to the abolition of the death penalty. In 1873, Giuseppe Zanardelli attempted to rework the proposals so as better to integrate the Sardinian and Tuscan penal codes, while also taking into account recent work in penal science on the question of criminal responsibility. But he fell from office before he was able to present this project to Parliament. Efforts by a later minister of justice, Savelli, to present a revised version of Zanardelli's first project also proved ineffective.[12]

Zanardelli had more success with his earlier project after his return as minister of justice in 1887. After making a few revisions, the new project was presented to Parliament. By July 1888, it had won the approval of both the Chamber and the Senate. In 1889, the code was promulgated by a royal decree, and it went into effect on 1 January 1890.[13]

The Zanardelli code, as it came to be known, established a new scale of punishments in Italy. The most notable change was the abolition of the death penalty. Italy thus became one of the first European states to eliminate capital punishment. The most severe type of punishment, reserved for those who had committed crimes like regicide and premeditated murder, was life imprisonment (*ergastolo*). The final version of the code decreed that the first seven years of this sentence would be spent in cellular isolation, with the obligation to work in the cell. After that, the inmate could move onto work in common during the day, under the rule of silence, with cellular segregation only at night. The preferred type of labor for the *ergastolani* was public works that would benefit the state. Parole was not possible, and amnesty was the only way a person sentenced for life could be released.[14]

The standard punishment for most crimes was imprisonment (*reclusione*) for a minimum of three days and a maximum of twenty-four years. A person sentenced to less than six months could spend his sentence in cellular isolation in a custodial prison. If the sentence exceeded six months, he was sent to a penitentiary (*casa di reclusione*) where he was placed under the progressive system of prison discipline. This required the inmate to spend at least one-sixth of his sentence, or up to three years, in cellular isolation. He could then move onto work in common, under the rule of silence, with cellular segregation only at night. Those incarcerated for more than three years were eligible to move onto an agricultural or industrial intermediate prison if they had served at least one-half of their sentence and had a good conduct record. After completing up to two-thirds of the sentence, an inmate with a good conduct record was eligible for parole.[15]

Running parallel to this type of imprisonment was a less severe form, detention (*detenzione*). This was reserved primarily for political criminals and those who did not display "depraved" instincts when they broke the law. Judges were not given the freedom to choose whether or not a criminal could be sentenced to *detenzione* instead of *reclusione*, primarily because detention was considered an exceptional punishment. The inmates were also subjected to a less severe disciplinary regime. They did not undergo an initial period of cellular isolation, for example, and they also had more choice in the type of work they could do while in prison. But they were not eligible for passage to an intermediate prison.[16]

The least severe type of imprisonment under the new code was simple arrest. This punishment was reserved for people who had committed petty crimes. The sentence, usually less than one year, was served exclusively in a custodial prison. Even though the longstanding goal of a unified penal code had at last been achieved, the Zanardelli code did not win the unanimous support of Italy's criminologists. Not surprisingly, the fiercest criticism of the new penal code came from members of the positive school of criminology. After seeing that Zanardelli's project reflected few, if any, of the ideas of the criminal anthropologists, Cesare Lombroso was moved to pen a polemic against the new code. Written in a mere eight days, this work, *Troppo presto*, was distributed to numerous deputies before the scheduled parliamentary debates in an ultimately futile attempt to stop the passage of the new penal code.[17]

Lombroso managed to find a few praiseworthy reforms in the new penal code. He agreed that prisoners should be required to work during their incarceration. He also liked the idea that Italy's most dangerous criminals would be sentenced for life and placed in separate institutions. He further applauded the punishment decreed for alcoholism, and he praised the reduction of the age of criminal responsibility from twenty-one to eighteen years, noting that some 31,085 crimes had been committed by men aged eighteen to twenty-one in 1885.[18]

He found much more to criticize in the code, however. Above all, he condemned what he termed its "excessive softness." As he saw it, many provisions in the code worked to the advantage of the accused and the convicted criminal rather than to the victim of crime and to society at large. Lombroso objected, for example, to the stipulation that if an attempted crime failed, the punishment would be reduced by one-sixth. He argued that the code should stipulate punishment for people who threaten to commit a crime, even if they fail to complete it, because born criminals often boasted of their future crime prior to committing it. To protect society and prevent crime, these born criminals must be stopped before they actually commit a crime.[19]

Lombroso also disputed the code's definition of a recidivist as one who committed the same type of crime more than once. He maintained that the statistics on crime (e.g., in England) proved that habitual criminals who had first committed a violent crime turned most often to property crimes for their second offense. As he saw it:

> The criminal who commits the same crime repeatedly is, almost always, a semi-imbecile, who has less need to be stopped by increasing the punishment; on the other hand, he who, after a short amount of time, commits a different type of crime, clearly has greater intelligence and versatility in crime, and has not just one single criminal impulse, but many.[20]

And these more intelligent, habitual criminals learned new criminal tricks while in prison. Indeed, said Lombroso, the prison "transformed" them from violent criminals into criminals against property.[21]

Lombroso also contested the abolition of the death penalty. Like Ferri, he argued that the death penalty was society's method of "natural selection." He maintained that nothing could be done for born criminals, those savages in society, "so that by destroying them, we save not only ourselves but also prevent the birth of beings more ferocious and sad than they."[22] Lombroso also argued that the retention of the death penalty would deter some types of crimes, particularly violent crimes against prison guards. He therefore urged that the death penalty be maintained as a "sword of Damocles" over the heads of prisoners who contemplated murdering a prison guard.[23]

Lombroso maintained that the "softness" in the penal code reached "dangerous" proportions with regard to the prison system. In his opinion, the Zanardelli code was emerging "too soon" and was doomed to failure unless it was preceded by extensive prison reform. In particular, he pointed out that Italy lacked the requisite number of cells to fulfill the dictates of the Irish system of prison discipline. Attempts to employ prisoners in public works and land reclamation projects would also prove inadequate because these types of work required the corrupting influence of a contractor or impresario.[24] If the country did not want the new code to be a "dead letter," it would have to approve the funds required to improve the prison system.

Lombroso also questioned the institution of parole. Using English statistics to support his case, he showed that many parolees actually returned to a life of crime. He thus called for parole to be used sparingly, and only after the intermediate prisons had been built and were functioning. He did not think parole should be extended to thieves, the "least corrigible" of all criminals, nor to recidivists of any sort.[25]

Finally, Lombroso asserted that Italy was simply not ready for a unified penal code. Stating that the country had achieved "unity but not unification," Lombroso noted that the different regions of Italy had diverse customs, sexual tendencies, and of course, different types of criminal behavior. Accordingly, the ideal penal code for Italy would not be a single unified code, but rather a set of different codes, each responding to the needs of the different regions of the country.[26]

In the parliamentary debates on the project in June 1888, Ferri predictably echoed Lombroso's criticisms of the Zanardelli code. Like Lombroso, Ferri depicted the code as soft on criminals. The elimination of the death penalty, he argued, forced a general diminution of penalties. The replacement of capital punishment with life imprisonment for crimes like regicide forced the legislator to reduce the punishment for simple murder, once punishable with death, to twenty-years imprisonment. Using English statistics to support his case, he shared Lombroso's disdain for the principle that the intensity of the punishment was more important than the length of the punishment.[27]

Ferri also saw the code as coming "troppo presto," particularly in view of the lack of prison reform. He argued that prison reform must precede the publication of the penal code; otherwise, the code would remain a "dead letter." Ironically, said Ferri, people have blamed the lack of a unified penal code for the slow pace of prison reform and the outright failure of the limited legislation on prison reform, such as the 1864 law requiring the construction of custodial prisons. But now, he believed, people would say that Italy had the code but lacked the money for prison reform, thereby guaranteeing the failure of the code. Furthermore, Italy's prison personnel were inadequately trained to oversee the "very delicate machine of the progressive system."[28]

In his impassioned discourse to the Chamber, Ferri reiterated his longstanding conviction that the government seemed more concerned with the welfare of the criminals than with the victims of crime. The institution of parole, for example, revealed that the government wanted to soften imprisonment but made no corresponding effort to help unemployed honest workers. He stressed the need for reparations to the victims of crime, underlining his point with a description of a recent visit to a penitentiary, in which he saw chickens roasting in the kitchen for sick inmates while honest workers went hungry on the streets.[29]

Despite his fervent pleas for the victims of crime, Ferri found few supporters either for his ideas or for the ideas of the positive school of criminology in the Chamber. Granted, some deputies agreed that prison reform should precede the publication of the penal code, or at least begin immediately thereafter. They recognized, however, that the cost of the needed improvements would most likely be prohibitive. A few deputies also voiced concerns about the institution of parole in Italy's criminal justice system.[30]

But most deputies disagreed with Ferri's claim that the penal code was excessively lenient. Panattoni, for example, pointedly told Ferri that Italy's prisons were far from being the places of ease that he implied they were:

> I have heard you lament that the prisons are too expensive for the state. Well, honorable Ferri, you have spoken of the excessive comfort of the prisoners . . . but you have certainly never visited the *ergastolo* of Foce, nor that of Linguetta and Favignana. There, in the darkness of those caves, you have not studied the man, forever left to his conscience and remorse: in those living tombs, in the solitude and silence that will last his lifetime, he will never hear another sound except the waves breaking against the rocks.[31]

In a similar way, Pietro Nocito argued that life imprisonment was harsher than the death penalty, as he had seen prisoners in Tuscany who, after five to six years in cellular isolation, could no longer perform such a simple task as purchasing a train ticket.[32]

Numerous deputies also spared no words in their condemnation of the new positive school of criminology. Identifying themselves as members of the classical school of criminology, they attempted to discredit Ferri's criticisms of the code by openly attacking the precepts of the positive school. Alessandro Fortis was particularly critical of the new school, calling it a pseudoscience. He pointed out, for example, that some of the physical anomalies that characterized Lombroso's notion of born criminals, such as a "receding forehead," were often seen in "normal" people. He argued that until the positive school developed clearly defined criteria needed to identify criminal man, it could not expect to influence the new penal code.[33]

Zanardelli, the minister of justice, similarly dismissed Ferri's criticisms of the project. He maintained that the code was not too lenient but rather followed the example of modern codes in Britain and Russia toward a general reduction in penalties. Zanardelli also completely disagreed with the notion that prison reform should precede the publication of the new code. The code provided the guiding principles for prison reform and thereby saved the country needless expense, he argued. He further maintained that the cost of prison reform would remain a pressing problem in Italy whether or not the new code was passed. Thus, the projected expense of the prison reform outlined in the new code should not be used as an excuse to reject the code.[34]

In the end, the positive school of criminology had to accept the Zanardelli code. After more work was done by several parliamentary committees, the final code was promulgated by royal decree on 30 June 1889. It went into effect on 1 January 1890 and would remain Italy's penal code until 1930.[35]

A new public security law, sponsored by Crispi, quickly followed the final approval of the Zanardelli code. This new legislation made several important revisions in the rights of public assembly and the use of admonition (*ammonizione*) and enforced domicile (*domicilio coatto*). It also reflected Crispi's previously stated goal to increase the preventive measures to stop crime before it began. It required, for example, that a group planning to stage a public protest must notify the public security forces at least twenty-four hours prior to the meeting. The law also clarified the previously vague provisions regarding when and how a person could be admonished or placed under enforced domicile.[36]

A new law on prison reform was an even more important requirement once the new penal code had been approved. Italy's prison system had to be adapted to the standards of the new code, particularly the Irish system of prison discipline, which required more cellular prisons and intermediate prisons. Indeed, upon the opening of Parliament in January 1889, King Umberto I stated his hope that legislation on prison reform would be presented to parliament as soon as possible.[37]

Crispi fulfilled his pledge to introduce a law on prison reform in March 1889. His goal of presenting a comprehensive bill on prison reform proved a practical impossibility, however, and he was forced to restrict the proposal to three key aspects of prison administration—buildings, prison guards, and the maintenance of prisoners.[38]

The prison buildings were Crispi's primary concern. Both the custodial prisons and the penitentiaries, particularly in southern Italy, needed extensive and costly renovations. Above all, new cellular prisons had to be built and sanitary conditions improved. Crispi proposed streamlining the expenses of the prison administration and applying the savings to the costs of renovation and construction of the prisons. He argued that this system was preferable to an annual allocation of funds because it would weigh less heavily on the country's already troubled finances. Such savings would result from the anticipated reduction of time prisoners would spend in prison, and from the sale of existing prison buildings that could not be adapted to the requirements of the new code.[39]

Crispi also suggested changes in the employment and hiring of prison guards in an effort to improve the security of Italy's custodial prisons. First, he wanted to use state rather than local employees for these posts. But he quickly stressed that this would not cost the government more money because these local jails would employ retired prison guards in exchange for room and board. Second, Crispi called for the reduction of the number of years a guard was required to serve before retiring—viz., from twenty-five to twenty years. He anticipated this reform would help the government keep the prison guards for a full career instead of having so many leave after their first contract service of seven years.[40]

The projected law also included several other provisions. Crispi proposed that the communes take over the maintenance of the prisoners in local jails. The state would continue to pay all costs in other types of prisons. To oversee the discipline and maintenance of Italy's prisons, Crispi called for the creation of a prison council made up of local dignitaries and prison officials. He argued that the benefits of this council would far outweigh its costs. He also underlined the need for the expansion of patronage societies throughout Italy. Finally, the law provided for the abrogation of the 1864 law that had required the construction of cellular custodial prisons throughout Italy.[41]

Crispi's proposal met sustained criticism in the Chamber, particularly from Deputy Achille Fagiuoli of Verona. His main complaint was that the proposed law, as presently designed, was too ambiguous. Crispi needed to clarify the costs of the projected prison reform, as well as give a better sense of the extent to which Italy's prisons needed renovation.[42] As it stood, Crispi seemed to be asking the Chamber to sign a blank check, an idea which struck Fagiuoli as alien to parliamentary government:

> It seems to me that Parliament, especially in questions of money
> . . . should try to know . . . at least briefly, the debt that the
> treasury would assume with the passage of this law. . . . And I say
> and repeat this, not to contest the debt which we must assume,
> but to stress that a legislative assembly in a free state should not
> blindly support and assume heavy financial burdens without first
> understanding why.[43]

Ferri shared Fagiuoli's belief that the proposed law gave too much power to the executive at the expense of Parliament. He also recognized that the law was rather vague and really addressed the needs of only the smaller custodial prisons. But he did not believe that the summary of projected expenses requested by Fagiuoli would facilitate prison reform. Indeed, the projected budget for the 1864 law on prison reform had proved worthless because Parliament had consistently failed to approve the required funds. Ferri speculated that it would take approximately thirty to forty years to complete the prison reform called for in Crispi's proposal. As a result, the new penal code would remain little more than pieces of paper for the next few decades.[44]

Several other deputies voiced similar reservations about the project. Prinetti, for example, argued that it placed too great a financial burden upon Italy's small towns and villages. He also believed that these small villages should have a voice in the process of prison reform. Finally, he asserted that the Prison Council would be a needless expense that would ultimately serve no purpose.[45]

Crispi dismissed these criticisms as unfounded.[46] Nevertheless, a parliamentary commission revised the proposed law so that the state rather than the communes would assume the cost of the construction and maintenance of the smaller custodial prisons. Crispi accepted this important modification, but he successfully pressed the Chamber to force the communes to pay for the cost of religious services and the day-to-day upkeep of the custodial prisons. After some debate, the law was finally passed on 22 June 1889 by a vote of 152–36.[47] It won the approval of the Senate a few days later and became law on 30 June 1889.[48]

The success of the new law on prison reform led Crispi to ask Beltrani-Scalia, the director general of the prisons, to compose a set of general regulations for Italy's prison system. In the 891 articles of the *Regolamento generale degli stabilimenti carcerari e dei riformatori governativi*, Beltrani-Scalia fulfilled an enduring goal to classify every aspect of the prison administration, from the duties of the prison personnel and the inmates to the proper organization of prison labor and accounts. The result was a highly centralized system in which all functions of the prison service were ultimately dependent on and subordinate to the director general and the Ministry of the Interior.[49]

The first part of the *Regolamento*, consisting of 219 articles, detailed the different types of penal establishments in Italy. The prison system was broken down into three types of penal institutions—preventive, ordinary, and special. The preventive prisons, reserved primarily for those awaiting trial, included the approximately fifteen hundred custodial prisons across Italy. The ordinary prisons, or the various prisons for convicted inmates, included the *ergastolo*, the penitentiaries (*case di reclusione*), and the detention homes (*case di detenzione*). The special prisons included a variety of institutions, most notably the asylums for the criminally insane and the intermediate prisons. To improve the efficiency of the prison bureaucracy, these prisons were grouped by region into three districts that were then divided into thirteen departments.[50]

The first part of the general regulations also outlined the duties of the prison personnel, including the prison guards. A brief look at the responsibilities of the prison director reveals the degree of subservience and obedience expected of the employees of the prison administration. The prison director was the eye of the director general in each prison and was called upon to oversee every detail of the institution. He was expected to know all of his employees and inmates and to serve as a role model "both in his public and private life" (Article 65). He ruled like a king in his small domain, the prison. But he was simultaneously completely subject to the authority of prison administration. He could not, for example, leave his residence for a day without permission of the local prefect or the minister of the interior. Moreover, he was required to submit detailed reports on all aspects of his prison according to a rigidly defined timetable. And, of course, he was not permitted to release any information or alter any aspect of the general regulations without the permission of his superiors. In sum, he was expected to be more a functionary who rigidly enforced the rules than an imaginative administrator who responded to the individual needs of the prison personnel and inmates.[51]

The approximately 5,280 prison guards were placed under an austere regime that paralleled the discipline of the inmates. The corps was divided into thirteen brigades that corresponded to the thirteen districts in the prison system. The guards were organized in a military-style hierarchy, and "subalterns" were required to give unquestioning obedience to their superiors. No guard could marry until he had served at least eight years with an unblemished record, and only then if he and his fiancée had the means (at least three thousand lire) to support a family. Free time was limited to two hours each day, and one-half a day every two weeks. A scale of punishments, ranging from a simple reprimand to expulsion from the service, covered every conceivable violation of the rules.[52]

The next 345 articles detailed the proper treatment and maintenance of the inmates in all types of penal establishments. In establishing these rules, Beltrani-Scalia declared that he was trying to create an environment that encouraged inmates to turn away form a life of crime:

> This first moment—this first step that an individual makes in the unhappy life of the prison, can often decide his entire future. And therefore, nothing will be spared to make him feel the severe but benevolent atmosphere in which he finds himself.[53]

Thus, when a person entered an *ergastolo* or a penitentiary (*casa di reclusione*), he was to be interrogated, searched, issued a uniform, and given a haircut, bath, and medical checkup. He was then placed in cellular isolation for either seven years or one-sixth of his entire sentence. As stipulated by the penal code, those sentenced to detention or simple arrest bypassed this period of cellular isolation.[54]

After completing the period of cellular isolation, the inmates moved on to work in common, under the rule of silence. Cellular segregation would take place only at night. During this period, inmates were divided into three classes—trial, ordinary, and merit. After a minimum of six months in the trial class, a prisoner who had earned enough merit points from the Disciplinary Council (consisting of the director, chaplain, physician, and a lower rank employee) could move on to the second or ordinary class. Again, after a period of six months, an inmate with enough merit points could move up to the third class, the merit class. Inmates in this category were eventually eligible to transfer to an intermediate prison.[55]

The prisoners were subjected to a strict disciplinary regime that was intended to strip them of their pasts, reeducate them, and prepare them for an honest life. They were called only by their number, not by their name, and they were expected to behave in a properly deferential manner toward their superiors. An inmate could not speak without permission, and he was required to answer in a low voice any questions put to him. Singing, playing cards, and writing on the walls were strictly prohibited. The use of tobacco was closely regulated and often forbidden. Convicted prisoners were not permitted to read "political books and journals" (Article 269). Violations of these and the many other prison rules could result in a variety of punishments, ranging from a simple reprimand to solitary confinement with a diet of bread and water. If prisoners behaved in a violent manner, they could be placed in a straitjacket or chains.[56]

The final two sections of the *Regolamento* outlined the norms for the budget and the accounting procedures for each type of penal establishment. Beltrani-Scalia emphasized the importance of these procedures, given the fact that the prison administration had an annual budget of approximately thirty million lire and oversaw an average of sixty-nine thousand prisoners every year. This service covered the norms for the purchase of prison uniforms, the acquisition of primary materials for the prison workshops, and the specifications for the construction and renovation of all types of prisons. It also administered the payroll of the prison guards and the approximately forty-eight thousand inmates who worked.[57]

The *Regolamento* thus offered a comprehensive system of control over Italy's prison system. But it was much easier to write rules than to enforce them. Beltrani-Scalia had recognized this difficulty, noting that even though the penal code and the general regulations required all convicted prisoners to work, this goal would not be easily accomplished. The inmates, most of whom came from an agricultural background, were ill-prepared to undertake industrial work. The prison administration also faced the continued protests of free workers who perceived the employment of convicts as a threat to their own jobs. The rules on prison labor would thus have to be compromised if not completely ignored.[58]

But thanks to Crispi, the legislation necessary for the much-needed reform of Italy's criminal justice system had, at last, been achieved. Parliamentary deputies and prison officials could no longer declare that prison reform was impossible. The legislation would remain a "dead letter," however, unless the Italian government could find the money necessary to complete the reforms.

Notes

1.   Crispi sponsored a number of other "progressive" reforms during his first premiership, including the Public Health Act of 1888 and the extension of voting rights at the local level. But his primary interest during this period was, of course, foreign policy, particularly the Triple Alliance and colonial expansion. For more information on the controversial figure of Francesco Crispi, consult Massimo Grillandi, *Francesco Crispi* (Turin: UTET, 1969); Mack Smith, *Italy*, 137–170; and Giorgio Candeloro, *Storia dell'Italia moderna* (Milan: Feltrinelli), vol. 6, *Lo sviluppo del capitalismo e del movimento operaio*, 336–373.

2.   See chapter 3.

3.   "Atti parlamentari: Discussione del bilancio della spesa del Ministero dell'Interno per l'esercizio finanziario, 1887–1888, 19 May 1887," *RDC* 17 (1887): 256–258.

4.   Ibid., 259.

5.   Ibid., 261.

6.   Ibid., 267–273. Prinetti (1851–1908), from Milan, was elected to the Chamber of Deputies in 1882 and sat with the deputies of the extreme Right. He is best known for his efforts to improve Italo-French relations in the early 1900s.

7.   Ibid., 275.

8.   Ibid., 275.

9.   Ibid., 276.

10.   Ibid., 276–277.

11.   See above, chapter 3.

12.   On the efforts to unify the penal code after 1865, consult Spirito, *Storia del diritto penale italiano*, 252–253; and Pessina, *Il diritto penale in Italia*, II: 734–735.

13.   Pessina, *Il diritto penale*, 735–736; and Mack Smith, *Italy*, 140.

14.   Ugo Conti, *La pena e il sistema penale del codice italiano* in *Enciclopedia del diritto penale*, ed. Enrico Pessina (Milan: Società Editrice Libraria, 1910), IV: 151–163; and Pessina, *Il diritto*, II: 740–742.

15.   Conti, *La pena*, IV: 219–235.

16.   Ibid., IV: 238–248.

17.   Lombroso-Ferrero, *Cesare Lombroso*, 264–265.

18.   Cesare Lombroso, *Troppo presto: Appunti al nuovo progetto di codice penale* (Turin: Bocca, 1888), 11–13.

19.   Ibid., 16.

20.   Ibid., 18.

21.   Ibid., 19.

22.   Ibid., 22–26.

23.   Ibid., 27.

24.   Ibid., 52–55.

25.   Ibid., 47–52.

26. Ibid., 62–66.

27. Enrico Ferri, *Sul nuovo codice penale: Discorsi alla Camera dei Deputati* (Naples: Luigi Pierro, 1889), 31–39, 71–72.

28. Ibid., 47.

29. Ibid., 55–59.

30. Italy. Camera dei Deputati, *Lavori parlamentari del nuovo codice penale italiano: discussioni della Camera dei Deputati (dal 28 maggio al 9 giugno 1888)* (Turin: UTET, 1888), 59–61, 107, 145–146.

31. Ibid., 91–92.

32. Ibid., 167.

33. Ibid., 295–297. Fortis (1841–1901), was elected to the Chamber in 1880 and served as Crispi's undersecretary of state for the interior, 1887–1890.

34. Giuseppe Zanardelli, *Discorsi parlamentari* (Rome: Tip. Camera dei Deputati, 1905), II: 248–259.

35. Pessina, *Il diritto*, 735–736; and Mack Smith, *Italy*, 140.

36. For more information regarding this new legislation, see Jensen, 140–146. For a copy of the new law, see "Legge sulla pubblica sicurezza," *RDC* 19 (1889): 354–362.

37 "Riforma penitenziaria," *RDC* 19 (1889): 34.

38 Chamber of Deputies, 28 March 1889, "Disegno di legge presentato dal Presidente del Consiglio, Ministero dell'Interno Crispi—Sulla riforma penitenziaria," *Atti parlamentari, Documenti—Disegni di legge—Relazioni*, 171, N. 78, 1–2.

39. Ibid., 2–3.

40. Ibid., 4–5.

41. Ibid., 5–6.

42. "Atti parlamentari: Discussione sulla prima lettura del disegno di legge per la Riforma penitenziaria," *RDC* 19 (1889): 245–246.

43. Ibid., 247.

44. Ibid., 254–258.

45. Ibid., 262–265.

46. Ibid., 274–277.

47. "Atti parlamentari: Discussione sulla seconda lettura del disegno di legge per la Riforma penitenziaria (14 giugno 1889)," *RDC* 19 (1889): 363–409.

48. Ibid., 409–411.

49. *Ordinamento generale della amministrazione carceraria* (Rome: Tip. delle Mantellate, 1891), VII–VIII. Beltrani-Scalia wrote a lengthy preface to this work, addressed to Crispi, that explained the various articles in the *Regolamento*.

50. *Regolamento generale degli stabilimenti carcerarii e dei riformatorii governativi* (Rome: Tip. delle Mantellate, 1891), 7–34. The prison system was divided as follows:

1st District:

1st Department—Belluno, Padua, Rovigo, Treviso, Udine, Venice,

Verona, Vicenza;
2nd Department—Bergamo, Brescia, Como, Cremona, Mantova, Milan, Pavia, Sondrio;
3rd Department—Alessandria, Cuneo, Genoa, Massa, Novara, Porto Maurizio, Turin.
2nd District:
4th Department—Arezzo, Florence, Grosseto, Leghorn, Lucca, Pisa, Siena;
5th Department—Bologna, Ferrara, Forlì, Modena, Parma, Piacenza, Ravenna, Reggio Emilia;
6th Department—Ancona, Ascoli, Macerata, Perugia, Pesaro;
7th Department—Rome;
8th Department—Aquila, Chieti, Teramo;
9th Department—Cagliari, Sassari.
3rd District:
10th Department—Avellino, Benevento, Campobasso, Caserta, Naples, Salerno;
11th Department—Bari, Foggia, Lecce, Potenza;
12th Department—Catanzaro, Cosenza, Reggio Calabria;
13th Department—Caltanissetta, Catania, Girgenti, Messina, Palermo, Siracusa, Trapani.
For more information, see *Ordinamento*, IX.

51. *Regolamento*, 38–47; *Ordinamento*, XXXVII–XXXVIII; and Guido Neppi Modona, *Carcere e società civile* in *Storia d'Italia* (Milan: Einaudi, 1973), V: 1922.

52. *Regolamento*, 81–108; Neppi Modona, 1922–1923.

53. *Ordinamento*, LXVI.

54. *Regolamento*, 111–211; Neppi Modona, 1924–1925.

55. *Regolamento*, 172–183.

56. Ibid., 123–136.

57. Ibid., 259–388; *Ordinamento*, CXXXI–CXLV.

58. *Ordinamento*, LXX–LXXVII. For evidence of the continuing disputes between the prison administration and free workers, see "La concorrenza al lavoro libero," *RDC* 19 (1889): 222–231.

7

A Dead Letter: Prison Reform in the 1890s

Italy's prison reformers began the last decade of the nineteenth century with renewed hope and vigor. After years of waiting, the required legislation and regulations were at last in place for a comprehensive transformation of Italy's prison system. But it was much easier to write laws and rules than to enforce them. Unfortunately, legislation emerged during the most turbulent decade of the young state's life. Even worse, the country's difficult financial situation throughout the 1890s forced the government to suspend funds intended for prison reform. Just as the positive school of criminology had predicted, the failure to adapt the prison system to the Progressive system of prison discipline led, in turn, to the limited application of the Zanardelli penal code. The lack of money also compromised the general regulations of the prison system because they, too, had been written in anticipation of the gradual implementation of the Progressive system of prison discipline. The heralded prison reform thus proved to be no reform at all, and by the turn of the century, calls were being made in Parliament for an investigation of the prison system and a reformulation of the prison regulations.

It is a commonplace that the 1890s were a decade of crisis for Italy. Internationally, the attempt to establish an empire in Africa culminated in the disaster at Adowa in 1896. Domestically, the country endured the banking scandals in 1892, the riots in Sicily (*fasci siciliani*) in 1893–1894, and the riots in Milan and the rest of the country in 1898. The decade ended with the famous debate on the *Statuto* and with Luigi Pelloux's near dictatorship.[1]

But it was Italy's dire economic situation in the late 1880s and early 1890s that worked against the success of the law on prison reform. By the late 1880s, the country was running a large deficit, thanks partially to a steady increase in spending on public works and the military. The disastrous tariff war with France after 1888 further exacerbated the situation. By 1890, Italy was confronting a deficit of almost 500 million lire and the government was forced to make hard choices between foreign and domestic policy.[2]

Given this situation, it is not surprising that the government opted to continue its glamorous colonial adventures rather than spend precious funds to improve the lot of the prison population.[3] Parliament began to restrict the funds required for prison reform soon after the passage of the law on prison reform in July 1889. Giovanni Giolitti, the new minister of the treasury, was intent upon reducing the budget by cutting spending rather than raising taxes. His declaration that "we must prepare a radical transformation of our prisons, without which the high ideals that inform our new penal legislation will be frustrated," did not exempt the prison system from the policy of economy. In the proposed budget for the Ministry of the Interior, presented in May 1890 to the Chamber of Deputies, almost two million lire were cut from the budget of the prison administration. The consequence was, of course, that no real progress would be made that year in constructing and renovating prisons according to the new progressive system of prison discipline.[4]

The key blow to the success of prison reform occurred in April 1891 when articles eight, nine, and eleven in the law on prison reform were suspended as part of the government's effort to balance the budget. These three fundamental articles had created a system of using the surplus amount from the annual prison budget for the construction and renovation of Italy's prisons. It had been anticipated that this surplus would be derived from a variety of measures, including a policy of economy in the prisons, the sale of existing prison buildings, and the profits of prison labor.[5] But the budget committee had recommended in December 1890 that "in view of the general condition of the finances," these surplus funds should be diverted to pay the costs of maintaining the prisoners for the following year.[6]

These actions were taken even though statistics underlined the desperate need for prison reform. In 1891, the minister of the interior, Giovanni Nicotera, admitted that the country had only 1,374 cells for continual segregation, and 1,360 cells for nightly segregation. The vast majority of the 18,696 places available in Italy's penitentiaries were in communal prisons. To fulfill the dictates of the penal code and the progressive system of discipline for long-term prisoners, Nicotera estimated that the country needed to build 4,743 cells for continual segregation and 26,730 cells for nightly segregation. The needs were just as great for the short-term prisoner, as the country needed to build 8,536 cells for cellular segregation and 14,445 for nightly segregation.[7] And the Ministry of the Interior estimated that it would need more than 80 million lire to complete this work.[8]

Leone Romanin-Jacur recognized that the suspension of these three articles jeopardized the successful application of the new penal code. In his presentation of the budget of the Ministry of the Interior to the Chamber in May 1891, he offered the popular argument that the difficult financial situation demanded so many sacrifices from honest folk that they could not be blamed if they did not try to improve the conditions of the prison population. He also implied that Italy should not rush to overhaul its prison system since other industrialized nations had taken decades to complete the transformation of their prisons. But he was forced to admit that his "technical people" had informed him that without prison reform, the punishments demanded by the new penal code would remain unfulfilled. Although the government could likely guarantee the completion of the works in progress, the funds for the future construction and renovation of the prisons would require the imagination of the Chamber.[9]

It was a new deputy in the Chamber, the noted legal expert Luigi Lucchini, who demonstrated most clearly that the penal code would remain unrealized without extensive prison reform. During the discussion of the proposed budget for 1891–1892, Lucchini stressed that the only aspect of the penal code that was adequately provided for was the punishment of life imprisonment (*ergastolo*). The progressive system of prison discipline would have to be compromised because two thirds of all prisoners were forced to spend their entire sentence in communal prisons. The country also lacked the special institutions that were required by the new penal code, such as those for habitual alcoholics and for juvenile delinquents.[10]

Lucchini perceived two key reasons for failure of prison reform and the consequent "nonrealization of the penal code." First, he blamed Italy's misguided ambition to great power status as a costly and dangerous threat to Italian public security:

> When one discusses this part of the budget, he must not only think of the financial aspect of it, but also and above all the moral side, the moral balance of the state, which precisely in this service reflects and finds it greatest development. We spend much money on the prospective wars against hypothetical enemies, but we do not provide adequate funds to fight as effectively as we should the true and real enemies that exist in our house.[11]

But he also charged that the state of the prisons stemmed from "an inertia, a decay that afflicts our administrations."[12]

Lucchini then offered several suggestions to improve the current state of the prisons. Saying he would be "crazy" to expect a dramatic and sudden change, given the state of the country's finances, he proposed that Parliament begin anew, trying to work out a realistic financial proposal for prison reform that would fulfill the basic requirements of the penal code. In the meantime, the government should develop a series of transitional and temporary provisions that would "reconcile the existing conditions of our penal establishments with the requirements of the law." To this end, he envisioned, for example, limiting cellular segregation to just a few types of prisoners rather than to all. He also called for the transfer of the prison administration from the Ministry of the Interior to the Ministry of Justice.[13]

The gloomy financial picture did not stop the promulgation of five royal decrees after 1891 authorizing the construction and renovation of a number of prisons, especially in southern Italy. The Ministry of the Interior, with the approval of the Ministry of Justice, recommended enlarging the custodial prison of Palermo, and transforming the penitentiaries of Viterbo and Augusta into cellular prisons. The prison administration also recommended that the penitentiary (and former *bagno penale*) at Nisida be converted from a communal prison into a cellular prison because "prisons that conform to the prescriptions of the new penal code do not exist in the southern provinces."[14]

These decrees proved unrealistic. Both the Ministry of the Interior and the Ministry of Justice had stressed in 1892 that the financial conditions of the state would dictate a slow and gradual transformation of the prisons. The general accounting office alerted the Prison Administration in April 1893 that the money for these projects was simply unavailable, given the decision to divert funds to the maintenance of the prisoners. The office thus maintained that the authorization of new projects was simply "vain and useless."[15]

The failure of the law on prison reform also guaranteed the limited application of the general regulations of the prison system. Granted, the prison administration attempted to enforce the detailed regulations to the letter. The central administration instructed the prison directors, for example, to refuse inmates' requests for supplemental food or permission to write home more frequently. They were also ordered to prohibit prisoners from wearing their own clothing or from having more frequent visits.[16] In practice, however, the austere regulations proved little more than a veneer on the existing system of prison discipline in both the penitentiaries and the custodial prisons.

The lack of suitable facilities constituted the key difficulty in the consistent application of the general regulations. In writing the *Regolamento*, Beltrani-Scalia had operated under the erroneous assumption that the prisons would be adapted to the progressive system of prison discipline. He also anticipated a degree of uniformity across the peninsula. He thus anticipated that all types of inmates would spend at least part of their sentence in cellular isolation. But as seen above, only twenty-four custodial prisons and eight penitentiaries met the requirements of the Zanardelli penal code. As the entire system had been designed with this idea in mind, it simply made the enforcement of other regulations even more difficult, if not impossible.[17]

The directors of both the custodial prisons and the penitentiaries consistently lamented the evils of life in common. The director of the penitentiary of Padova argued, for example, in his annual report for the year 1896–1897, that the large rooms which held approximately 700 inmates (676 in this period) were "unsanitary and immoral" and should be abolished. Even worse, the large dormitories promoted numerous disciplinary problems. With only eighteen cells to segregate possible violent or threatening inmates, the director noted that the only recourse he would have in a riot or a threatening situation would be to shoot the inmates. He further argued that such a prison revolt was a real possibility because the furnishings of the large rooms provided the inmates with all the materials they would need to build a barricade.[18]

The director the penitentiary of Piombino reported that his communal prison also promoted numerous disciplinary problems. This prison, which included a section for the final or intermediate stage of prison discipline, was also a communal facility. The director noted, however, that the division of prisoners into several classes had led to a decline in disciplinary infractions. But the design of the building prevented him from rewarding the prisoners as stipulated by the *Regolamento*. They could not be given extra time for rest or walks, nor provided with light in their cells, as they had none. The director argued that he was forced to compromise the rewards due the well-behaved prisoners because the communal prison design demanded, for safety's sake, that the inmates be kept on a rigid timetable of walking, waking, and sleeping.[19]

The situation in the custodial prisons was even more difficult, as the *Regolamento* stated that the accused and the convicted were required to remain separate. Yet in prison after prison across the peninsula, the accused mixed freely with the convicted. The director of the custodial prison of Melfi, for example, reported that the design of the prison made it impossible to adopt the prescribed treatment for the different types of prisoners. The directors of the custodial prisons of Catanzaro, Palermo, and Piacenza likewise reported that the design of these prisons hindered segregating prisoners according to sex or offense. They also found it impossible to stop the use of tobacco and to employ the prisoners in a productive occupation.[20] Although the problem predominated in the South, an inspection of the custodial prison of Mantova revealed that prisoners were not segregated according to sex or age and that they regularly violated the rules about dress, talking, and smoking.[21]

Even cellular prisons presented difficulties. In Perugia, where a custodial prison for continual cellular segregation had been erected in 1865, complaints were made about the impact of continual cellular isolation on the prisoners. In the 266 cells, which held 146 convicted inmates and 49 accused, the prison doctor suggested in 1896–1897 that keeping prisoners in cells for twenty-three hours a day contributed to chronic illness among the inmates. Furthermore, the prison director noted it was difficult to find a place where the prisoners could work together.[22]

The requirement that all prisoners work while incarcerated also proved to be another unenforceable requirement of the general regulations. The prison administration tried to fulfill this promise by employing workers in a variety of trades, especially shoemaking, carpentry, and weaving. They also did not restrict themselves to just state management of prison labor, but also permitted use of the contract system of prison labor.[23]

The attempts to employ prisoners met with difficulties, thanks to a combination of poor facilities and the lack of contracts. The penitentiary of Fossano, for example, was able to employ fewer than one-half of its inmates. The prison had 94 looms employing 150 prisoners, but the work steadily declined during the 1890s as the government contracts with the Army dried up. The prison director tried to get employment for 40 carpenters, but his efforts did not succeed because the prison administration would not adapt the building to the contractor's specifications. The only contract work that proceeded well was shoemaking and basketweaving, but that employed only 90 of the 499 inmates.[24]

The penitentiary of Spoleto experienced similar problems. In late 1899, only 123 of the 414 inmates were employed. It was anticipated that the employed would drop by about 65 in the next few months, as the contracts employing the shoemakers and the tailors were coming to an end. An inspector of the prisons, G. Berardi, predicted that employment in the prison would continue to decline as industry became increasingly mechanized.[25]

The fear of competition between free workers and prison laborers also continued to inhibit the growth of prison industries. Throughout the 1890s, free workers regularly petitioned the administration with requests and demands to stop providing work to prisoners. In April 1900, for example, a committee of five cobblers in Alghero presented themselves to the office of the subprefect to demand that the penitentiary of Alghero stop underselling them in the local marketplace. But the prison director maintained that even if the shoemaking ended, the local cobblers would not gain any advantage because the local population would simply buy similar items in Sassari.[26]

The penitentiary of Augusta experienced similar complaints from local workers. In November 1899, the Società Filantropica Liberale Umberto I of Augusta met specifically to discuss the question of free and prison labor. The results of the meeting were sent to the Ministry of the Interior and revealed that the local workers, particularly the cobblers, cabinetmakers, and furniture makers, saw the prison as a threat to their livelihood. In almost hysterical terms, they argued that the prison had initially limited its work contracts to the government but had then gradually encroached on their trades. The impact had proved disastrous for the local working class because the local elite, lured by cheap prices, had begun to buy or contract goods from the penitentiary "without regard for the quality or solidity of the work." The workers argued that they could not compete effectively with the prison because the prison administration supplied the raw materials and, of course, the labor was cheap. Given this trend, the workers predicted an eventual monopoly of all industry in the area, even of "the manufacture of bread and pasta." Claiming life was difficult enough without the competition from the prison, the free laborers demanded that the prison stop selling its goods locally and stop obtaining contracts for work from local citizens.[27]

This protest had the desired effect. Although the director of the prison tried to argue that the alleged competition was greatly overstated, and that the prisoners were obligated to work according to the penal code and prison regulations, the prison administration told him in no uncertain terms to stop selling products locally "in view of the excessive competition with free industry." This order plunged the prison workers into enforced idleness, and the cobblers, furniture makers, and cabinetmakers were completely devoid of work. The prison director's attempt to restore employment in April 1900 to the shoemakers was again denied because of the fear of "serious disorder by free workers."[28]

The Chamber of Deputies also regularly confronted the question of free versus prison labor. In May 1891, the Radical deputy Felice Cavallotti spoke for many of his colleagues when he declared that he found it difficult to accept that the government ministries provided work to prisoners when so many free workers were unemployed. The minister of the interior, Giovanni Nicotera, reminded Cavallotti that employment of prisoners reduced disciplinary problems. But he too was moved to say that certain types of work, such as the employment of prisoners to print the *Gazzetta ufficiale*, would be better entrusted to free workers.[29]

The debate reemerged at the end of the decade. The Socialist deputy Andrea Costa, who had earlier attacked prison labor, demanded that the minister of the interior, Luigi Pelloux, agree to a resolution that would effectively close down the printing press in the Rome prison, *Regina Coeli*. Pelloux refused, and during a discussion in December 1899, he stressed that only fourteen prisoners were employed in the binding and folding of the journal. The rest of the work was done by free laborers. Considering the small number of prisoners employed, he argued that free workers would gain minimal advantage if the work in the prison ended. And in a swipe at the Socialists, Pelloux noted that the government would not risk the possibility of a strike with the publication of the *Gazzetta ufficiale*. In the end, the prison administration continued its publication of the journal, although several deputies continued to declare that all the problems with this official publication, such as lack of quality, would disappear if the prison administration was removed from supervising its publication.[30]

Other aspects of the general regulations also came under heavy criticism throughout the decade. The prediction that the rations would be insufficient proved true.[31] Prisoners frequently complained that the food was inadequate, and a common request to a prison director was for supplemental rations. The director of the penitentiary of Nisida noted, for example, that one of the prisoners' most frequent requests was the "need for extra food because of hunger."[32] And the poor quality of the food, as well as the small amount, resulted in a riot among the inmates at the penitentiary of Pallanza.[33]

Visitors to the prisons confirmed that the rations were inadequate. Adolfo Zerbaglio, a professor of law at the University of Pisa, visited several penitentiaries (Volterra, San Gimignano, Piombino, Lucca, Portolongone, Portoferraio) with the permission of Beltrani-Scalia. He found that the food and bread were of decent quality but that "the daily ration of food is excessively small" and inadequate for the good health of the prisoners.[34] Another visitor to the custodial prison of Cagliari, Dr. Tommaso Anchisi, found the prisoners emaciated and clearly hungry.[35] And Jesse White Mario, on a visit to the penitentiary on the island of Procida, found the food good "though scant."[36]

The "complementary institutions" created by the general regulations also failed to develop and function properly during the 1890s. The visitors' committee, made up of local notables and politicians, was expected to serve as an independent regulatory body for the prison administration. It was required to visit the local penal establishment at least once a year to make sure that the regulations were being followed properly and to entertain the complaints of the inmates. At the end of each fiscal year, the committee was supposed to send an annual report to the prison administration. Yet throughout the decade, prison directors across the peninsula reported that the visitors' committee rarely, if ever, fulfilled its duties.[37]

The patronage societies (*società di patronato*), founded to aid prisoners immediately after their release, also met with limited success. These patronage societies obviously served a two-fold purpose. On the one hand, they could help prisoners find employment and thus avoid a return to a life of crime. On the other hand, they permitted continued surveillance of released prisoners. For these reasons, Beltrani-Scalia had argued that the patronage societies were the most important of the complementary institutions created by the general regulations.[38]

Only sixteen patronage societies existed prior to 1889, all located in central and northern Italy. In December 1889, Crispi called upon the prefects to encourage the creation of such societies in all provinces.[39] Beltrani-Scalia made a similar appeal in May 1891.[40] But even though a number of patronage societies were set up by the end of the decade, they existed in name only in many southern cities. The groups in Girgenti, Salerno, and Caserta, for example, were created after 1890, but failed to function throughout the decade. In cities like Brescia and Florence, where patronage societies had existed before 1889, the number of patrons dropped steadily throughout the 1890s, perhaps victims of the economic problems of the decade.[41]

The personnel entrusted with managing the prisons and guarding the prisoners also contributed to the failure of the general regulations. Beltrani-Scalia had created a hierarchy of personnel in which everyone, from the lowest-level guard up to the director of the prison, was expected to give unquestioning obedience to his superiors. They were also expected to obey the rules and regulations without deviation unless they had received express permission from their superiors.[42]

In practice, however, the personnel rarely lived up to the expected level of obedience and professionalism. The guards, in particular, came under continuous criticism from the prison management. In their annual reports, the prison directors regularly lashed out at the guards for sleeping while on duty, drunkenness, and familiarity with the prisoners. The director of the penitentiary of Fossano, for example, asserted that most guards were inept and unable to maintain the discipline of the prison. He noted also that some guards were revealing their confidential orders to the prisoners.[43]

The inspectors of the prisons of the realm reported similar failings among the prison guards. Inspector Eugenio Sampò, for example, blamed the chief guard Ferdinando Zanni for the disorder that prevailed in the custodial prison of Mantua in early 1900. Sampò maintained that Zanni's continued neglect of his duties had given the prisoners free rein in the prison. He also found that he accepted gifts from the families of the prisoners in exchange for lighter duties and failed to provide prisoners with the salary and clothing they were due.[44] Inspector Giuliano Berardi likewise found the guards at the penitentiary of Alghero in early 1897 to be "bad, undisciplined, riotous, and dedicated to wine and restlessness."[45]

The guards were almost universally blamed whenever an inmate escaped. The flight of two long-term inmates from the custodial prison of Cagliari was attributed to the guards' having given help to the prisoners. An attempted escape from the custodial prison of St. Maria Capua Vetere in Naples in 1896 was attributed to the negligence of the guards, and disciplinary action was recommended. Similarly, an attempted breakout from the custodial prison of Catanzaro led a prison inspector, Aristide Bernabò Silorata, to recommend that several guards be disciplined.[46]

Most prison directors attributed the inadequacies of the prison guards to their lack of culture and education. They also argued, as did the director of the penitentiary of Padua, that the guards were more interested in their salaries than in the prison service:

> The prison guards . . . once nearly formed a special caste, and were once all trustworthy and able guards; but now, many enroll in the corps of guards only because they cannot find better work. The corps of guards has lost and continues to lose that myth and spirit that gave it strength, respect, and bravery, as the service is no longer important, the knowledge of duty, . . . that pride that

pushes a man to don the uniform that links him to the prison
guards; no, but only, the paycheck, and having money to spend
on amusements. They are always ready to quit the service, not
only when they hope to improve their lot, but also when they see
a chance for something new.[47]

The prison directors called for higher standards of recruitment to eliminate the
persistent difficulties with the guards. The director of the penitentiary of Fossano
demanded a continuous purge of the guards with the goal of eliminating the habitual
drinkers, "ladies' men," and those heavy in debt.[48] The director of the penitentiary
of Padua intimated that the current preference given to ex-soldiers was not wise
because they were accustomed to obey superiors in uniforms, not those like the
prison management dressed in civilian clothing.[49]

To improve the prison guards, several directors also recommended a
substantial revision of the regulations that governed the corps of guards. A common
suggestion was that the guards be given permission to marry after a certain period
of time. As the director of the penitentiary of Fossano noted, "this restriction does
little more than promote mistresses and increase the number of illegitimate
children." There were also several suggestions to give the guards better pay, more
time off, and permission to wear civilian clothing outside the prison.[50]

The Ministry of the Interior acknowledged the demanding nature of a prison
guard's life. In response to a query from Parliament, the Ministry noted that the
lack of liberty, social prejudice against the guards, and poor working conditions
contributed to problems in retaining guards. Indeed, the prison administration
suffered a shortage of guards during the 1890s. In 1891, for example, 5,136 guards
were employed but 5,353 were needed. With a prison population that hovered
around 70,000, there was just one guard for every fourteen prisoners.[51]

Even though the prison administration recognized that the guards had reason
to complain, it responded with fear and hesitation when the prison guards made an
independent effort to organize and improve their lot. In the mid-1880s, for
example, a newspaper for the guards was started. This publication, *La Guardia
Carceraria*, lasted for two years. It was forced to cease publication because its
straightforward presentation of the complaints and conditions of the prison guards
had "grated too strongly on the just susceptibilities of the superior directors."
Indeed, the director of the custodial prison of Cosenza had regularly confiscated this
newspaper because he found it "a subversive journal in which the bad guards
foolishly believe they find support and satisfaction against their superiors."[52]

La Guardia Carceraria became the standard by which other publications of
the guards were measured by the prison administration. A collaborator with this

journal, F. Capaccini, initiated a similar publication, *La Riforma degli Agenti di Custodia*, soon after the demise of *La Guardia Carceraria*. The stated goals of this new journal revealed the desire to improve working conditions, to gain greater respect, and to win greater autonomy and independence. These included the reduction of working hours, an increase in the premium for guards who reenlisted after the first seven years of service, the permission to wear civilian clothing during off-duty hours, an increase in the number of guards, the modification of prisons to make the work of the guards easier, and the creation of a separate infirmary for them. Capaccini stressed that the journal was not meant to create a gulf between the guards and prison management, and he noted that everything would be done in perfectly legal and gentlemanly fashion.[53]

But like the earlier journal, this new publication prompted expressions of concern from the prison management. The director of the custodial prison of Catanzaro, for example, found this journal too similar to *La Guardia Carceraria*, and as such, "greatly harmed the discipline of the corps of guards." Yet another journal, *Il Corriere Carcerario*, also aroused the suspicion of the prison director of Bari, who argued that its program sounded too much like the program for *La Guardia Carceraria*, "which was more intent on disrupting than maintaining the discipline of the corps." [54]

Different educational backgrounds and training help to explain the tension that obviously existed between the prison management and the prison guards. A person could not even apply for a job in the prison management without a law degree from one of Italy's universities.[55] Accountants and bookkeepers were also expected to have completed the necessary professional degrees and training. Guards, however, simply needed to know how to read, write, and do elementary arithmetic.[56] Furthermore, the prison directors were trained to expect unquestioning obedience from their subordinates, especially the guards. As the designated authority in the prison, it is not surprising that they preferred to institute reforms from above rather than have the guards agitate for them from below.

The day-to-day events in a prison were almost always presented from the point of view of the prison management because they were the ones who wrote the annual reports. They often seized the opportunity to praise their own work and that of their subordinates. But the inspections of the prisons revealed that prison directors also violated the general regulations. In mild cases, the director of the penitentiary of Spoleto was characterized as a moody hypochondriac in a penitentiary where disciplinary problems abounded.[57] In more extreme cases, an inspection of the custodial prisons of Naples in 1895 revealed that the director had failed in all aspects of his job. He only visited the prison once every two or three months, did not read the inmates' correspondence, and rarely gave audiences to the prisoners. He also used money gained from kickbacks or payments from inmates' families to purchase an expensive home and a carriage.[58] Even worse was the case of the director of the custodial prison of Messina. He was convicted and sentenced to six months in prison, along with other personnel, including the chief guard, for taking monthly payments from the supplier to the prison.[59]

At the end of the decade, accusations of brutality to inmates highlighted the problems with the prison personnel. In 1897, a reputed anarchosocialist, Romeo Frezzi, was arrested on suspicion of complicity in an attempt to assassinate King Umberto I. A few days after his incarceration in Rome's San Michele prison, he was found dead. In the same year, another inmate, Pietro Torres, charged that he had been beaten by guards while held in the prisons of Santo Stefano and Portolongone. In 1899, it was reported that another inmate in Santo Stefano had been beaten to death by the guards. During the same year, cries of inmates were reportedly heard outside of the custodial prison of *Regina Coeli*, in Rome.[60]

Not surprisingly, Socialist and Radical deputies led the charge in reporting these incidents to the Chamber and demanding an explanation from the government. Deputies Enrico Ferri, Oddino Morgari, and Filippo Turati, for example, demanded to know the cause of Frezzi's death. Morgari stressed that Socialists had a right to know what happened to Frezzi because the same might happen to Socialist deputies "in our frequent and numerous incarcerations."[61] As it turned out, the government did reopen the case. After an investigation, two policemen and three prison guards were arrested, but later released, for the crime.[62]

Deputies Matteo Imbriani and Ettore Socci, who presented the other accusations against the prison administration, demanded more than a simple explanation. In 1897, Imbriani called for an independent, non-governmental committee to investigate the Torres case. The minister of the interior, Antonio Di Rudinì, refused this request, much to the relief of the prison administration.[63] Socci's demand for a general investigation of Italy's prison system in 1899 was likewise refused by the prime minister and minister of the interior, Luigi Pelloux. Pelloux argued that such an investigation would bring discredit and dishonor to the entire prison administration.[64]

But by the end of the decade, the government was forced to admit the essential failure of prison reform. In his report to the Chamber on the budget of the Ministry of the Interior for 1898–1899, Deputy Bruno Chimirri revealed that Italy needed 16,619 cells for continual cellular segregation and 26,232 cells for nightly segregation in order to fulfill the dictates of the Zanardelli penal code. He estimated that the necessary construction would cost at least 82 million lire. Although he recognized that the financial condition of the state still prohibited sufficient funding for prison reform, he reiterated the old argument that money spent now would ultimately save money. In other words, effective prison reform would lead to a decline in crime and a corresponding decline in the need for prisons.[65]

This argument was ineffective, as approximately one-half of the budget of the Ministry of the Interior was already being funneled into the prison system.[66]

The following year, the director general of the prisons, Giuseppe Canevalli, confirmed the limited achievements of the prison administration. In a report to a governmental committee, he admitted that "we are not yet at the point where we can say, not even approximately, when such prison reform will be completed." Most custodial prisons and penitentiaries failed to meet the specifications required by law. In the penitentiaries, 25,138 of the 30,607 available posts for men were in communal prisons. Less than one-fourth of all inmates in custodial prisons spent even part of their sentence in cellular segregation as prescribed by law. Canevalli also lamented the lack of work available to the prisoners. In 1898, only 14,131 places were available in the prison workshops, with 11,448 more needed.[67]

The government and the prison administration thus realized that Italy's prison system remained unchanged in spite of the law on prison reform and the general regulations. In future years, the prison administration would be forced to redefine its priorities and needs. The general regulations would also have to be drastically redesigned in order to meet the realities of the existing state of the prisons. The failure of prison reform in the 1890s would make possible a more realistic approach to the renovation of Italy's prisons in the next decade.

Notes

1.   For a general overview, see Martin Clark, *Modern Italy, 1871–1982* (London: Longman, 1984), 92–118; and Mack Smith, *Italy: A Modern History* (Ann Arbor: Univ. of Michigan Press, 1969), 141–210. On the *fasci siciliani*, consult Francesco Renda, *I fasci siciliani, 1892–1894* (Turin: Einaudi, 1977). On the end-of-the-century crisis, see Giorgio Candeloro, *Storia dell'Italia moderna* (Milan: Feltrinelli, 1986), vol. 7, *La crisi di fine secolo e l'età giolittiana*, 11–93.

2.   Giorgio Candeloro, *Storia dell'Italia moderna* (Milan: Feltrinelli, 1986), vol. 6, *Lo sviluppo del capitalismo e del movimento operaio*, 360–373.

3.   It should be noted that there was a push in 1891 to create a penal colony in Italy's nascent colonial possessions, particularly Eritrea. Giuseppe Leti, writing in Enrico Ferri's journal, *La Scuola positiva*, argued that prisoners could pave the way for the free settlers to Eritrea. He also maintained that the long-term benefits of the colony would far outweigh the projected costs of setting up a penal colony. In Parliament, Deputy Rocco De Zerbi also called for the creation of a penal colony in Eritrea. But a governmental commission in 1891 determined, much to the relief of the director general of the prisons, Martino Beltrani-Scalia, that setting up a penal colony in Eritrea would be costly and perhaps harmful to discipline. In 1898, a short-lived experiment was made at Assab to set up a penal colony for those sentenced to enforced domicile, but after six months of high mortality rates for both the inmates and the guards, it was closed down. For more information, consult Giuseppe Leti, "Colonie penitenziarie all'Eritrea," *La scuola positiva* 1 (1891): 600–624; Martino Beltrani-Scalia, "La colonia Eritrea e la deportazione: lettera aperta all'on. Rocco De Zerbi, deputato al Parlamento," *RDC* 21 (1891): 165–173; and "Carceri e colonie penali nella Eritrea," *RDC* 21 (1891): 597–601.

4.   "Atti parlamentari—Camera dei deputati—"Relazione della Giunta generale del Bilancio sul disegno di legge presentato dal Ministro del Tesoro (Giolitti) il 30 novembre 1889," *RDC* 20 (1890): 331–341; and Giovanni Giolitti, *Memoirs of My Life*, trans. Edward Storer (New York: Howard Fertig, 1973), 61–64.

5.   "Legge sulla riforma penitenziaria," in Ministero dell'Interno, Direzione generale delle carceri, *Ordinamento*, 7–8.

6.   "Atti parlamentari—Camera dei deputati," *RDC* 21 (1891): 204–206.

7.   "Atti parlamentari—Senato del Regno—"Discussione sullo stato di previsione del Ministero dell'Interno," *RDC* 21 (1891): 377–385.

8.   "Rassegna parlamentare italiana," *Rivista Penale* (hereafter *RP*) XXXIV (July 1891): 57.

9.   "Atti parlamentari—Camera dei deputati—Stato di previsione della spesa del Ministero dell'Interno per l'esercizio finanziario 1891–1892," *RDC* 21 (1891): 260–261.

10. "Rassegna parlamentare italiana," *RP* XXXIX (August 1893): 162–165.

11. "Rassegna parlamentare italiana," *RP* XXXVI (February 1893): 178–179. Lucchini, as the editor of *Rivista penale*, noted earlier in a summary of the parliamentary debates that it would be better to spend Italy's limited resources on the prison system rather than waste them on "ridiculous colonial adventures." See "Rassegna parlamentare italiana," *RP* XXXIV (July 1891): 57.

12. "Rassegna parlamentare italiana," *RP* XXXIX (August 1893): 162–163.

13. Ibid., 165–167.

14. ACS, Ministero dell'Interno, Direzione generale delle carceri, 1893–1900, Busta 77. The director of the penitentiary of Nisida argued against such a renovation because it would mean the loss of four-hundred places in the penitentiary. See ACS, Ministero dell'Interno, Direzione generale delle carceri, Busta 18.

15. Ibid., Busta 77, Letter to the Ministero dell'Interno, Direzione generale delle carceri, 21 April 1893.

16. Ibid., Buste 1 and 2.

17. See, for example, Beltrani-Scalia's preface to the *Regolamento generale* in Ministero dell'Interno, Direzione generale delle carceri, *Ordinamento generale*, IX–CLIV. On the number of suitable prisons, see ACS, Ministero dell'Interno, Direzione generale delle carceri, 1893–1900, Busta 77.

18. ACS, Ministero dell'Interno, Direzione generale delle carceri, 1893–1900, Busta 18, Casa di Reclusione di Padova, "Relazione sull'andamento dei diversi servizi dell'anno 1896–1897, 23 August 1897."

19. Ibid., Busta 19, Casa di Reclusione di Piombino, "Relazione generale dei vari servizi di questa casa per l'esercizio 1892–1893."

20. Ibid., Busta 2.

21. Ibid., Busta 18, Carceri giudiziarie di Mantova, "Ispezione del Cav. Sampo, 6 aprile 1900."

22. Ibid., Busta 19, Carceri giudiziarie di Perugia, "Relazione annuale sull'andamento del servizio, 1896–1897, 30 settembre 1898."

23. Only the accused awaiting trial in the custodial prisons were exempt from this rule. See Ministero dell'Interno, Direzione generale delle carceri, *Regolamento generale*, 137–142.

24. ACS, Ministero dell'Interno, Direzione generale delle carceri, Busta 17, Casa di reclusione di Fossano, "Relazione annuale, 1896–1897, 31 luglio 1897."

25. Ibid., Busta 19, Casa di reclusione di Spoleto, "Ispezione, 25 settembre 1900."

26. Ibid., Busta 52.

27. Ibid., Busta 53.

28. Ibid., Busta 53.

29. "Atti parlamentari," *RDC* 21 (1891): 294–295.

30. The debate prompted an article in *La Stampa* (Turin) in December 1898, in which the author argued that the question of free labor versus prison labor always reached a fever pitch during times of high unemployment. *La Stampa* came down

on the side of the prison administration, arguing that prisoners indeed should have work for education, moral regeneration, and rehabilitation. It also noted that the Socialists who were trying to wrest the work away from the prisoners were thereby creating a situation in which they would have to pay all the costs of maintaining the prison population. But the newspaper left unresolved what type of work was best suited to the prison population. See "Il lavoro dei carcerati," *RDC* 24 (1899): 38–40.

31.   See Martino Beltrani-Scalia, "Il regolamento generale delle carceri," *RDC* 21 (1891): 445–453, for this and other criticisms leveled against the general regulations.

Prisoners in custodial prisons, lifers, and those in the first stage of ordinary imprisonment received 600 grams of "second quality" bread and soup once a day. Prisoners in the second stage of their sentence in penitentiary were given 600 grams of "ordinary" bread and soup once a day. A typical soup was made up of 120 grams of pasta, 10 grams of dried beans, 40 grams of vegetables, 12 grams of lard, 10 grams of salt, and 5 grams of onions. They were supposed to receive meat in their soup at least once a week. See Ministero dell'Interno, Direzione generale delle carceri, *Regolamento generale*, 397–400.

32.   ACS, Ministero dell'Interno, Direzione generale delle carceri, 1893–1900, Busta 18, Casa di reclusione di Nisida, "Relazione annuale, 1892–1893, 20 marzo 1894."

33.   ACS, Ministero dellInterno, Direzione generale delle carceri, 1893–1900, Busta 18, "Casa penale di Pallanza–Inchiesta, 12 dicembre 1896."

34.   Adolfo Zerbaglio, "Brevi appunti d'una gita penitenziaria," *RDC* 22 (1897): 537.

35.   Pietro Vasto, "Il vitto dei detenuti," *RDC* 25 (1900): 112–113.

36.   Jesse White Mario, "Crime and Politics in Italy," *The Nation* 55 (10 November 1892): 351.

37.   For the complaints of prison directors and prefects regarding the lack of visits, see ACS, Ministero dell'Interno, Direzione generale delle carceri, Buste 13 and 18. On the duties of the visitors' committee, consult Ministero dell'Interno, Direzione generale delle carceri, *Regolamento generale*, 30–33.

38.   Ministero dell'Interno, Direzione generale delle carceri, *Ordinamento generale*, xxiv–xxv; and Ministero dell'Interno, Direzione generale delle carceri, *Regolamento generale*, 23–30. It should also be noted that the patronage societies thrived on the idea that criminals were made by society and their environment, not born. Prison inspector Giustino De Sanctis, for example, stated in 1895 when presenting the constitution of the new patronage society in Pisa that he could not accept "the theory of the new school which holds that the great majority of criminals are insane or delinquent by nature." He maintained instead that his twenty-two years in the prison system had proved to him that the "born criminal" was the exception and the "made criminal" the rule. See ACS, Ministero dell'Interno, Direzione generale delle carceri, Busta 16 for more information. For a typical

constitution of a patronage society, see ACS, Ministero dell'Interno, Direzione generale delle carceri, 1893–1900, Busta 14, "Statuto della Società di Patronato in Macerata (1898)."

39. ACS, Carte Crispi, Rome, Scatola 19, Fascicolo 395 (232). This circular led to the establishment of organizing committees in several southern cities, including Naples and Benevento.

40. *Bulletino ufficiale delle carceri* 21 (1891): 154–155.

41. ACS, Ministero dell'Interno, Direzione generale delle carceri, 1893–1900, Busta 12. The number of patrons in Brescia, for example, dropped from a high of seventy-eight in 1889 to a low of thirty-five in 1896.

42. See chapter 5.

43. ACS, Ministero dell'Interno, Direzione generale delle carceri, 1893–1900, Busta 17, Casa di reclusione di Fossano, "Relazione annuale, 1896–1897, 31 luglio 1897."

44. Ibid., Busta 18, Carceri giudiziarie di Mantova, "Ispezione del Cav. Sampò, 6 aprile 1900."

45. Ibid., Busta 20, Casa penale di Alghero, "Ispezione, 24 giugno 1897."

46. Ibid., Busta 29.

47   Ibid., Busta 18.

48. Ibid., Busta 77.

49. Ibid., Busta 18.

50. Ibid., Buste 18 and 19.

51. "Atti parlamentari," *RDC* 21 (1891): 262–264.

52. ACS, Ministero dell'Interno, Direzione generale delle carceri, 1893–1900, Busta 6.

53. Ibid.

54. Ibid.

55. The examination for entrance into the prison management lasted two days. On the first day, each examinee was required to write a paper on an aspect of penal law. On the second day, the candidates were given oral exams, with questions on penal and civil law as well as Italian history and political economy. The aspirants also had to translate a passage from Italian into French. See *Ordinamento del personale amministrativo ed aggregato* in Ministero dell'Interno, Direzione generale delle carceri, *Ordinamento generale*, 1–47, for more details.

56. *Ordinamento del personale di custodia* in Ministero dell'Interno, Direzione generale delle carceri, *Ordinamento generale*, 56–57.

57. ACS, Ministero dell'Interno, Direzione generale delle carceri, 1893–1900, Busta 19, Casa di reclusione di Spoleto, "Ispezione–25 settembre 1900."

58. Ibid., Busta 18, Carceri giudiziarie di Napoli, "Ispezione, 16 dicembre 1895."

59. Ibid., Busta 18.

60. Ibid., Busta 33; Jensen, "Liberty and Order," 333–341; and "Atti parlamentari—Discussione del Bilancio dell'Interno (seduta del 5 dicembre 1899)," *RDC* 25 (1900): 12–13.

61. Indeed, both Morgari and Turati were arrested after the riots in Milan in 1898.

62. Jensen, "Liberty and Order," 334–335; and Chamber, 5 March 1897, *Atti parlamentari*, cum. vol. 570. *Discussioni*, 1: 349–351.

63. "Il bilancio del Ministero dell'Interno e la inchiesta nell'Amministrazione delle carceri," *RDC* 22 (1897): 387–389.

64. "Atti parlamentari, Discussione del bilancio dell'Interno (Seduta del 5 dicembre 1899)," *RDC* 25 (1900): 12–15.

65. "Atti parlamentari, Camera dei deputati, Relazione della Giunta generale del bilancio sullo stato di previsione della spesa del Ministero dell'Interno per l'esercizio finanziario 1898–1899," *RDC* 24 (1899): 34.

66. "Atti parlamentari, Camera dei Deputati, Discussione dello stato di previsione della spesa del Ministero dell'Interno per l'esercizio finanziario 1898–1899," *RDC* 24 (1899): 62–63.

67. "Commissione per la statistica giudiziaria, sessione dicembre 1899, Sulle condizioni degli stabilimenti penali in confronto col numero dei condannati," *RDC* 25 (1900): 213–225.

8

Prison Reform in the
Giolittian Era, 1901–1914

The Giolittian era, so often associated with economic improvement and political reforms, was a period of modest reform of Italy's prison system, at least on paper. Longstanding problems in the prison system, such as how and where to employ prisoners, were partially resolved. Other needed changes in the general prison regulations were successfully introduced. The improved financial condition of the country permitted a modest improvement in the standard of living for the prison personnel as well as the construction and refurbishment of several prisons. These improvements could not counteract decades of neglect or the social and economic disparaties of the kingdom, however. By the onset of World War I, the structure and material conditions of Italy's prisons were only marginally better than those in the prison system at the time of unification in 1861.[1]

The question of prison labor reemerged in the first decade of the twentieth century. The primary reform demanded in this period was the increased employment of prisoners in land reclamation, particularly in unhealthy, malarial sites. Beltrani-Scalia had advocated the use of prison labor in this manner in the 1880s, and in fact had realized a trial colony at Tre Fontane, outside of Rome.[2] The idea resurfaced during the 1890s. In 1891, the Royal Commission that explored the use of Eritrea for a penal colony maintained that it would be preferable to employ prisoners in land reclamation projects on the peninsula rather than sending them to Eritrea. Indeed, the commission recommended sending free workers to labor in the "healthy and fresh climate of the high plain of Abyssinia," whereas prisoners would be relegated to the "unhealthy climate of our uncultivated lands."[3]

The Zanardelli penal code, as well as the general prison regulations, presented difficulties in the realization of this idea. Inmates were only supposed to be permitted to work in penal agricultural colonies after they had served part of their sentence in cellular segregation and when they had developed a good conduct record. In 1893, Luigi Lucchini called for Parliament to modify the penal code and prison regulations in ways that would ease the employment of prisoners in land reclamation projects and agricultural labor.[4]

The director general of the prisons, Giuseppe Canevalli, also recommended the use of inmates in land reclamation projects. In his report of 1898, he lamented the lack of work available to the prisoners. He revealed, for example, that the prison workshops had 14,131 places, but that 11,448 more were needed. Given the continuing problems with free workers, he advocated using more prisoners in land reclamation projects. He argued that this work would achieve the dual goal of stimulating prison reform and improving Italy's agricultural production, the "first formation of the riches of our country." He proposed revising the existing regulations to make it possible for long-term prisoners to work on such projects. Rather than use penal agricultural colonies as rewards for good behavior, one should use them, and especially those in "unhealthy locales," as part of the punishment of long-term prisoners.[5]

The Giolittian era would finally see the implementation of this idea. In November 1900, the minister of justice, Emmanuele Gianturco, presented a project to the Chamber calling for the employment of prisoners in the reclamation of "uncultivated and unhealthy lands." To convince his audience of the need to reform the system, Gianturco underlined the essential failure of prison reform up to that point, and the consequent non-realization of the penal code. The reasons for this situation were twofold—the lack of adequate facilities for cellular segregation and nightly segregation, and the difficulty in finding work for the prisoners. Indeed, Gianturco stressed that approximately one-third of all inmates were simply idle from lack of work. He argued that these idle prisoners also violated the spirit of the penal code: "work must form the main element in the atonement of every punishment that restricts personal liberty, and the efficacy of this work stems less from its difficulty and more from its type." Gianturco then maintained that his proposed law would fulfill the twin goals of permitting all prisoners to spend at least part of their sentence in cellular segregation and in working. Regarding cellular segregation, he called for the introduction of a temporary measure to reduce the required amount of time in such segregation from one-sixth to one-twelfth of the sentence. As he saw it, this would reduce the average number of prisoners in cellular segregation to 1,789. Since the country had 2,328 available cells, no more money would have to be spent on their construction. Such a reduction in cellular segregation would also benefit the inmates, as statistics indicated a higher suicide and death rate among inmates in cellular segregation.[6]

Gianturco offered four reasons for the employment of prisoners in land reclamation projects. First, it was difficult to find work for the current prison population. The prison administration, for a variety of reasons, including untrained personnel and inadequate raw materials, was unable to win contracts for its inmates. Second, free workers constantly complained about the perceived unfair competition with prison laborers. Third, since 55 percent of the prison population came from agricultural backgrounds, and only 8 percent were currently employed in agricultural projects, the government was converting this vast population into mediocre craftsmen. Fourth, the prison administration could claim real success at the existing penal agricultural colonies, especially those in Sardinia. To dispel fears regarding mass escapes of dangerous criminals working out in the open, Gianturco argued that the presence of mounted guards would deter prisoners from trying to flee the work site. [7]

A few months later, Martino Beltrani-Scalia offered a proposal in the Senate to employ prisoners in the reclamation of the *Agro romano*. He proposed allocating part of the annual budget of the prison administration to the work of prisoners in this land reclamation project. Like Gianturco, he used the same argument to justify non-industrial employment—viz., most prisoners were agricultural laborers prior to their incarceration—an argument he had used several years before to develop support for Tre Fontane.[8] To drum up support for his idea, Beltrani-Scalia later outlined the benefits of the employment of prisoners in the reclamation of the Agro romano. He repeated many familiar arguments, stressing the fact that most prisoners came from agricultural backgrounds. He also discounted the population's fear that thousands of prisoners would encircle Rome. Beltrani-Scalia maintained that the prisoners would be easier to control than the "free agricultural laborers who would make their way into Rome at the first hint of danger." Finally, he dismissed the idea that the prisons would be left empty and useless and that the prisoners would pose a threat to the livelihood of free agricultural laborers.[9]

When Gianturco's proposal fell through, Giolitti presented an alternative project to the Chamber in December 1902. Essentially, Giolitti sought the approval of the Chamber for prisoners to bypass the second stage of the progressive system and move onto work in the open. If the number of inmates performing land reclamation still proved insufficient, he proposed a future reform that would abbreviate the period of cellular segregation. Regarding possible objections like mass escapes, Giolitti pointed to the statistics from Tre Fontane to stress that this would not be a problem. He also answered questions regarding the health and mortality rate in land reclamation, stating that recent health measures (e.g., quinine use) would cut down on the number of problems.[10]

Luigi Lucchini presided over the parliamentary commission that studied Giolitti's proposal. In presenting his report in June 1903, he largely reiterated the reasons for bypassing the penal code and permitting inmates to work in the open. He also stressed that most prisoners came from agricultural backgrounds and consequently benefitted little from learning industrial trades. The goal of the commission was to permit a wide variety of inmates to work in "cultivation and reclamation" until the necessary facilities existed to meet the requirements of the penal code.[11]

By March 1904, the law had won approval in the Chamber. The project was then sent to the Senate where Giolitti again summed up the benefits of permitting prisoners to reclaim malarial lands:

> The realization of this proposed system will restore equilibrium to these numbers. It will erase the appearance of even partial competition with free industry; it will remove a considerable number of prisoners from enforced idleness; it will restore the agricultural laborers and workers to their natural profession; and it will lower the cause of tuberculosis and restore uncultivated lands to the country.[12]

Despite some reservations from the Senate committee, the proposal passed the Senate and became law on 26 June 1904.[13]

This reform certainly enjoyed the enthusiastic support of Italy's working class. Almost immediately after Giolitti came to power, cobblers and other artisans demanded either limitations on or an elimination of work for prisoners. In 1903, for example, the prefect of Porto Maurizio had informed the Ministry of the Interior that the cobblers of Oneglia were complaining that the contractor in the local penitentiary was pursuing unfair pricing practices. It is thus not surprising that in March 1904, a committee of workers endorsed Giolitti's plan to employ the prisoners in land reclamation. But they wanted the proposal to go even further, and employ inmates in agricultural work on a grand scale. They claimed that agricultural work would serve the dual purpose of rehabilitating the prisoners and eliminating their threat to the livelihood of the industrial working class.[14]

But as with so many other pronouncements on prison reform, this law also proved difficult to realize. Less than a year after its passage, Lucchini lamented in the Chamber that the law remained, like so many other Italian laws, a "dead letter." He complained particularly that the funds required to implement the basic requirements of the law had not been provided for after its passage. He argued it was crucial to implement this law because the abundant number of idle prisoners must be employed, and the unequal treatment of prisoners across the peninsula must end.[15]

The director general of the prisons, Alessandro Doria, confirmed that the prison administration was still awaiting the funds for the project. He thought that perhaps the Chamber had mistakenly believed that the prison administration could divert funds from its ordinary budget to pay the costs of the new project. An unanticipated shortage of prison guards in 1905 had also slowed the development of the penal agricultural colonies, especially in Sardinia, as Doria pointed out. Moreover, towns with prisons slated for closing had raised loud protests at the prospect of losing the employment opportunities the prison supplied to their communities.[16]

The early Giolittian era also saw the first substantial revisions of the general regulations of the prison system. In the Chamber, Pilade Mazza led the assault on the general regulations. He depicted them as barbarous and uncivilized, primarily because corporal punishment was the basic method for enforcing the disciplinary regime of both the inmates and the employees. He called, first, for the reform of the philosophy behind these rules and then for the renovation of Italy's prison system. Giolitti responded by claiming that prisons were, above all, places of punishment. He recommended, however, that humane measures must be used in the punishment of inmates and employees.[17]

Guglielmo Curli echoed Mazza's criticism of the general regulations. In a critical study of the prison system, Curli decried the regulations as too harsh and too structured. He compared the regulations to a chemistry textbook in that they were over-written and over-structured. Consequently, it was impossible to treat the inmates as individuals. He maintained that the prison regulations should be flexible enough to accord special or specialized treatment to individual inmates. In other words, inmates must be treated and diagnosed, and not simply submitted to a preplanned regime. He also lamented the continued use of chains and straitjackets in Italy's prisons. In European states like Belgium, he declared, those objects were in museums.[18]

The first revision in the rules was prompted not by these complaints but rather by a longstanding parliamentary demand that all prisoners be subjected to the same disciplinary regime. The prison regulations of 1891 had stipulated that inmates sentenced to *lavoro forzato* under the previous penal code were still required to wear the heavy chains that had been mandated in the regulations of 1878. Several prison directors regularly complained to the prison administration that it was impossible to fulfill this requirement.[19] These same inmates had also been permitted to continue other activities, such as cooking their own food during religious festivals. The prison administration seized the opportunity to ban this special treatment, to limit the number of walks, and to restrict access to a number of items, such as glass and extra clothing, that were not permitted in the new regulations.[20]

A more important revision in the general prison regulations resulted from the dramatic events of May 1903. A young prisoner, Giacomo D'Angelo, was found suffocated to death in a straitjacket (*camicia di forza*) in the prison of *Regina Coeli* in Rome. As the facts emerged, it became apparent that D'Angelo had not been convicted of any crime and in fact had been subjected to the extreme treatment of the *camicia* for over forty-eight hours.[21]

Public outcry was swift and vociferous. The Socialist newspaper, *Avanti!*, led the attack on the prison administration and on the general prison regulations. In the ensuing months, demands were made for a revision in the stipulated treatment of difficult and violent inmates, as well as the punishment of the prison director and the prison guards. When the trial was finally held in October and November 1903, *Avanti!* followed the proceedings closely, reporting testimony on a daily basis.[22] But in the end, the opponents of the prison administration were disappointed, when the director of *Regina Coeli* and other prison personnel were absolved "for lack of any crime."[23]

The prison administration termed the sentence a victory. The Socialists gathered a group of workers to protest the decision. But, in fact, the entire episode forced major revisions in the general prison regulations. In reporting the changes to the minister of the interior, the general director, Alessandro Doria, noted that the recent "most terrible episode" had prompted the creation of a committee to explore "possible improvements" in the general prison regulations.[24]

The committee recommended fundamental changes in the system of punishment for inmates. Essentially, it called for a reduction in the "intensity and length" of the current scale of punishments. In particular, it demanded the abolition of all types of "instruments of physical coercion and torture, such as the *camicia di forza* and chains." Violent prisoners could be restrained with a safety belt (*cintura di sicurezza*), but only upon the approval of a physician. Furthermore, punishment for other disciplinary infractions would be reduced. Prisoners who disobeyed prison personnel, for example, would now be subject to temporary segregation instead of five to fifteen days in isolation with a diet of bread and water. A prisoner guilty of numerous disciplinary infractions would only be punished for the most severe of those violations.[25]

The committee also seized the opportunity to revise the manner of classifying prisoners in the general prison regulations. The system of points, or merits and demerits, used to group prisoners into classes, had long been criticized by outside observers and prison directors. The latter group found it difficult to define a demerit, much less a merit, given the fact that they did not observe all inmates on a regular basis. Consequently, the committee decided to return to the system used in 1878 in the general regulations of the *lavori forzati*. Merits would no longer be considered in the movement from one class to the next. Rather, each inmate would progress to the next class depending on the amount of time he had been imprisoned and the number of demerits on his record. Only disciplinary infractions could retard an inmate's progress to the next class. Overall, Doria argued, these changes would make life easier for both the prison directors and the inmates. It would also help eliminate the frequent meetings of the Council of Discipline.[26]

This new decree compelled numerous prison directors to write the prison administration for clarification. They reminded Doria of the difficulty in enforcing the regulations, given the lack of work and the poorly trained guards.[27] Indeed, two circulars, one in 1902 and the other in 1903, on "blood crimes" detailed the violence endemic in Italy's prisons and indicated the futility of the general regulations. They underlined the lack of stability and disorder in the prisons and tried to consider all types of violence in the prisons.[28]

Members of Parliament, and particularly the Socialists, were also unmoved by the revisions in the general prison regulations. Filippo Turati, himself an ex-prisoner, delivered a bitingly accurate picture of the Italian prison system. In his famous speech of 18 March 1904, Turati noted that the D'Angelo affair, like the death of Frezzi, had momentarily captured public attention. Demands had been made to change the system, and Doria and the prison bureaucracy had responded by modifying the prison regulations. But to Turati, this effort was meaningless. He maintained that a system that absorbed almost half of the yearly budget of the Ministry of the Interior required more than bandages when bleeding occurred. Calling the prisons of Italy "tombs," "slaughterhouses," and "houses of corruption," Turati added his name to the long list of critics calling for a comprehensive overhaul of the prison system.[29]

Turati demanded that reform begin with the prison regulations. He did not believe that Beltrani-Scalia's regulations were totally devoid of merit, but he pointed out that the prison bureaucracy had found it much easier just to brutalize and intimidate the inmates into obedience. Turati further maintained that the regulations dehumanized the inmates. Prisoners were stripped of their past and their individuality and transformed into numbers. The regulations also made it impossible for inmates to maintain contact with their families. Furthermore, the rule of silence was a sinister attempt to destroy the spirit and individuality of the inmates. Consequently, "every provision instead, which concerns the duty of the State to provide for the redemption of the offender . . . remains a dead letter."[30] The prison schools, patronage societies, regular work, and even walks, thus remained largely unfulfilled.[31]

Turati blamed the prison personnel for many of the deficiencies in Italy's prisons. Turati characterized the prison director as a mere bureaucrat who made no real effort to become acquainted with the prisoners. Meetings with the inmates were deliberately rapid and meaningless, and held primarily for the annual report. The prison doctors and chaplains also failed the inmates because the guards prevented close communication between the two. Indeed, Turati argued that the prison guards, and not the prison personnel, really ran the prisons. These guards were uneducated and cruel:

> That man [the guard], meanwhile . . . is almost always a southerner, because it is only in the regions that lack industry that

one could find anyone inclined to take on this disgraceful, unpleasant, and odious job; and he is illiterate, or nearly so, and above all angry at everything and everyone, because his life is the life of a prisoner . . . and, like the prisoners, he lives his life in an environment of suspicion and mistrust, continually spied upon and punished, so that he turns his hatred on the prisoner, the only person who cannot respond.[32]

The prison administration obviously needed to address these problems but instead occupied its time compiling statistics. Repeating the old argument that these conditions contributed to Italy's "primacy" in crime, Turati concluded that it was a "sacred duty" of the government to develop once again a "prison program" and to begin the process of removing Italy's prisons from the Middle Ages.[33]

Turati continued his assault on the prison administration in April 1906. He again reiterated his criticisms of the Italian prison system—the decision of the government to concentrate attention on projects like railroads, because they affected the "galantuomini" rather than the sixty-thousand plus inmates, a "permanent population," who essentially had no political voice; the failure of general regulations in terms of their rehabilitative aspects; and the dehumanization of the inmates by means of the rule of silence in the "tombs of the living." But in this speech, Turati suggested several concrete reforms that he considered essential to the improvement of the Italian prison system. First, regarding the inmates, he called for a more humane approach:

> Abolish all dispositions that foolishly forbid any contact with the outside world, that forbid talks with relatives, or correspondence, or the reading of books, or of newspapers; all that residue of ferocious vendetta that demoralizes and does not improve anyone. [34]

Second, he demanded a comprehensive inquiry into the prison problem, modeled on the English prison reports. As he saw it, only extensive investigation would produce any long-term plans for reform. Finally, he suggested the transfer of the prison administration from the Ministry of the Interior to the Ministry of Justice. The Ministry of Justice would help eliminate the disciplinary, police-like nature of punishment in Italian prisons.[35]

The material conditions of the prisons certainly supported Turati's description of them as "living tombs." In July 1904, Doria presented a report on the state of the prisons to a judicial committee that echoed earlier reports on the state of the prisons. He noted in his introductory comments that little had changed in the material conditions of the prisons since the first such report in 1894. Like his predecessors, he blamed the essential lack of change on the inadequate funds allocated to the prison system. Indeed, throughout his report, Doria underlined the failure to adapt the prison system to the needs of the new penal code. Going hand in hand with this failure was, of course, the failure of the general regulations, as these rules had been formulated on the expectation of prison reform. The key problem remained the shortage of cellular custodial prisons. Italy still did not have enough cells for even one-half of the inmates.[36] The penal code could thus not be followed to the letter, and "one is constrained to tolerate a promiscuity that is damaging to the administration of justice and to discipline and hygiene."[37]

The yearly inspections and annual reports confirmed the lamentable material conditions of the prisons throughout the Giolittian era. An inspection of the custodial prison of Caltanissetta in 1906 revealed once again the longstanding problems with overcrowding and poor ventilation.[38]

The inspectors increasingly blamed the personnel of the prisons rather than poor material conditions for the perennial problems with discipline. As in the past, the prison guards came under heavy fire. The inspector of the custodial prison of Caltanissetta in 1909 revealed, for example, that the prison guards had clearly favored some inmates over others. Prisoners with ties to the *camorra* had predictably enjoyed the greatest favoritism because the guards feared possible inmate rebellions otherwise.[39]

But the inspectors also severely criticized the administrative personnel of the prisons. An inspection of the custodial prison of Nicastro in 1909, for example, revealed the incompetence of the prison director. He was found to be completely negligent in the enforcement of the regulations, permitting the prisoners to sing and mingle freely. The new vice-director of the prison of Turi was also found incompetent in 1911, preferring friends "devoted to games."[40] And an uprising at the penitentiary of Bergamo in 1912 was attributed to the former director of the prison, whose failure to enforce the general regulations during his tenure as director led to a violent uprising by the inmates in December 1912 when the new director tried to assert his authority.[41]

An inspection of the penitentiary of Finalborgo in 1912 yielded similar complaints about the director of that prison. He was found to be excessively soft in the enforcement of the disciplinary regulations, and he failed to hear the inmates' grievances on a regular basis. He was also accused of permitting the inmates to receive unauthorized books, including material of "sensational and pornographic subjects."[42] The director of the penitentiary of Fossombrone similarly fell under heavy criticism after an inspection. He was accused of failing to oversee the guards and for failing to keep orderly records in the prison.[43]

This heavy criticism was probably motivated by the scandals that plagued the prison bureaucracy throughout the Giolittian era. After the D'Angelo affair, another tale of brutality and inappropriate conduct emerged in 1906 at the *ergastolo* of Santo Stefano. This incident concerned the mistreatment of Pietro Acciarito, the man who had attempted to assassinate Umberto I in 1897. In the aftermath of this episode, Turati again lashed out at the prison system as "a blasphemy against civilization" and demanded a general parliamentary investigation of Italy's prison system.[44]

This study never took place, but the prison administration did make a few improvements in the material conditions of the prisons. In 1905, work was finally begun on a new custodial prison in Caltanissetta.[45] Parliament introduced legislation for the construction of a large new facility in Naples the same year.[46] A year later, the government announced plans to renovate a number of custodial prisons in southern Italy.[47]

The prison administration also tried to raise the standard of living of its personnel. It also revised the regulations that governed both the administrative workers and the prison guards.[48] But the changes were minimal. The guards had previously agitated for shorter working hours and more time off. In the new regulations, the guards were given an extra hour of free time. Otherwise, the new rules largely resembled the regulations of 1890. The treatment of the guards remained closer to that of the prisoners than that of the administrative personnel.[49]

But other than these limited achievements, the Giolittian period witnessed few, if any, substantial improvements in the Italian prison system. In 1907 and again in 1913, members of Parliament could still declare, in language remarkably similar to that of Federico Bellazzi, that Italy's prisons were more places of intimidation and fear than of rehabilitation and hope.[50] Little wonder that in 1915, the director general of the prisons, Gerardo Gerardi, informed the minister of the interior that Italy was years away from a comprehensive reform of its prison system.[51]

Notes

1.   On the economic and political successes of the Giolittian era, consult A. William Salomone, *Italy in the Giolittian Era: Italian Democracy in the Making, 1900–1914* (Philadelphia: University of Pennsylvania Press, 1960); and Giorgio Candeloro, *Storia dell'Italia moderna* (Milan: Feltrinelli, 1986), vol. 7, *La crisi di fine secolo e l'età giolittiana.* For an excellent biography of Giolitti, see Nino Valeri, *Giovanni Giolitti* (Turin: UTET, 1972).

2.   See chapter 4.

3.   "Carceri e colonie penali nella Eritrea," *RDC* 21 (1891): 599.

4.   Italy, Camera dei Deputati, *Indice generale degli Atti parlamentari* (Rome: Tip. Camera dei Deputati, 1898), I: 67.

5.   "Commissione per la statistica giudiziaria, sessione dicembre 1899, Sulle condizioni degli stabilimenti penali in confronto col numero dei condannati," *RDC* 25 (1900): 216–217.

6.   "Atti parlamentari, Camera dei Deputati, Disegno di legge presentato dal Ministro di Grazia e Giustizia e dei Culti (On. Gianturco) nella seduta del 22 novembre 1900, sul impiego dei condannati nei lavori di dissodamento e di bonificamento dei terreni incolti e malsani," *RDC* 26 (1901): 25–32.

7.   Ibid., 32–37.

8.   "Relazione dell'on. Beltrani-Scalia al Senato del Regno sulla proposta di legge per il bonificamento agrario dell'Agro romano," *RDC* 26 (1901): 161–166.

9.   Martino Beltrani-Scalia, "Il bonificamento dell'Agro romano con la mano d'opera dei condannati," *RDC* 26 (1901): 401–413.

10.   "Atti parlamentari, Camera dei Deputati, Disegno di legge presentato dal Ministro dell'Interno (on. Giolitti) nella seduta del 6 dicembre 1902, Sull'impiego dei condannati nei lavori di bonificazione di terreni incolti o malarici," *RDC* 28 (1903): 25–30.

11.   *Atti parlamentari. Documenti,* Legislatura XXI, 2 sessione, 1902–1904, N. 255A, 1–16.

12.   "Atti parlamentari—Senato del Regno—Disegno di legge presentato del Ministro dell'Interno (Giolitti) nella tornata dell' 8 marzo 1904 approvato della Camera dei Deputati il 3 della stessa mese—Impiego dei condannati nei lavori di bonificazione di terreni incolti e malarici," *RDC* 29 (1904): 158–161.

13.   For the royal decree, see *Bollettino Ufficiale delle Carceri* 29 (1904): 245–246.

14.   ACS, Ministero di Grazia e Giustizia, Direzione Generale degli Istituti di Prevenzione e Pena, Busta 243. For complaints about prison labor throughout the decade from cobblers in Elba, Milan, Pallanza, and Alghero see the reports in ibid., Busta 213, Busta 214, and Busta 14.

15.   "Atti parlamentari, Camera dei Deputati, Discussione sul bilancio del Ministero dell'Interno, tornata dell'8 aprile 1905," *RDC* 30 (1905): 238–241.

16.   "Statistica giudiziaria e notarile—Relazione presentata alla Commissione per la Statistica nella sessione del marzo 1906 sull'applicazione della legge 26 giugno 1904, n. 285, per l'impiego dei condannati nei lavori di bonificazione dei terreni incolti e malarici," *RDC* 31 (1906): 141–143. On the limited achievements of the penal agricultural colonies in the Giolittian period, see Italy,   Ministero dell'Interno, Direzione Generale delle Carceri e dei Riformatori, *La colonizzazione interno nelle sue applicazioni col mezzo delle Colonie penali agricole* (Rome: Tip. delle Mantellate, 1912).

17.   "Atti parlamentari, Camera dei Deputati, Tornata del 25 giugno 1901, Discussione del bilancio del Ministero dell'Interno," *RDC* 26 (1901): 289–292.

18.   Guglielmo Curli and A. Bianchi, *Le nostre carceri e i nostri riformatori* (Milan: Enrico Rechiedei, 1902), 9–77.

19.   So, for example, the directors of the prisons of Nisidia and Senigallia both expressed their disapproval of the continued use of chains on the *forzati*. See ACS, Ministero dell'Interno, Direzione generale delle carceri e dei riformatori, 1901–1905, Busta 68.

20.   See the royal decree dated 2 August 1902, as well as Giolitti's circular to the prison directors, dated 28 September 1902 in *Bollettino ufficiale delle carceri*, 227 (1902): 297–298 and 301–304.

21.   For the details of the case, see Ernesto Querci-Seriacopi, *Il passato, il presente, e l'avvento dell'amministrazione delle carceri in Italia* (Rome: Tip. delle Mantellate, 1925), 46; and "Tra gli ingranaggi della giustizia—l'omicidio D'Angelo nel carcere di Regina Coeli," *Avanti!* VII (6 Nov 1903).

22.   The testimony was summarized daily from 6 November to 2 December 1903.

23.   "Tra gli ingranaggi della...giustizia," *Avanti* VII (2 December 1903; and "La sentenza nella causa D'Angelo," *RDC* 28 (1903): 469. For a copy of the sentence, see "Causa D'Angelo," *RDC* 29 (1904): 174–188.

24.   "Leggi e Decreti," *Bollettino ufficiale delle carceri* 29 (1904): 1–3.

25.   Ibid., 12–20.

26.   Ibid., 7–10 and 20–24.

27.   ACS, Ministero di Grazia e Giustizia, Direzione Generale Istituti di Prevenzione e Pena, Buste 68 and 98.

28.   " Circolari," *Bollettino ufficiale delle carceri* 30 (1904): 409–410.

29.   Filippo Turati, *Discorsi parlamentari* (Rome: Tip. della Camera dei Deputati, 1950), I: 312–313.

30.   Ibid., I: 313.

31.   Ibid., I: 318–322.

32.   Ibid., I: 319.

33.   Ibid., I: 322.

34.   Filippo Turati, *Carceri—repressione dei tumulti e fondi segreti. Discorso presentato alla Camera dei Deputati il 3 aprile 1906* (Milan: Uffici della *Critica Sociale*, 1906), 15.

35. Ibid., 17.
36. "Sull'applicazione degli istituti penitenziari secondo il codice penale italiano e sui risultati di essa—Relazione presentata dal direttore generale delle carceri alla Commissione per la statistica giudiziaria e notarile (Sessione del luglio 1904)," *RDC* 31 (1905): 39–54.
37. Ibid., 55.
38. ACS, Ministero di Grazia e Giustizia, Direzione generale istituti di prevenzione e pena, Busta 108.
39. Ibid., Busta 106.
40. Ibid., Busta 424.
41. Ibid., Busta 424.
42. Ibid., Busta 425.
43. Ibid., Busta 426.
44. Turati, I: 475. On Acciarito, see Jensen, "Liberty and Order, " 327–330.
45. ACS, Ministero di Grazia e Giustizia, Direzione generale istituti di prevenzione e pena, Busta 547.
46. "Camera dei Deputati—Disegno di legge presentato nella seduta del 21 giugno 1905 dal Presidente del Consiglio . . . —Per la costruzione di un nuovo carcere giudiziario nella città di Napoli," *RDC* 31 (1905): 287. The prison was to have two thousand total places, including eighteen hundred cells.
47. "Atti parlamentari—Camera dei Deputati—Relazione della giunta generale del bilancio sul disegno di legge presentato dal Ministro del tesoro (A. Majorana), nella seduta del 29 novembre 1906," *RDC* 32 (1907): 85–87.
48. "Relazione a S.E. il Ministro dell'Interno sul regolamento per la carriera degli impiegati dell'amministrazione degli stabilimenti carcerari e dei riformatori governativi e del personale ad essi aggregato," *Bollettino ufficiale delle carceri* 29 (1904): 374–384.
49. "Relazione a S. E. il Ministro dell'Interno sul regolamento organico per il Corpo degli agenti di custodia degli carceri," *Bollettino ufficiale delle carceri* 29 (1904): 424–469.
50. See, for example, "Discussione del bilancio dell'Interno sui capitoli per l'amministrazione carceraria," *RDC* 32 (1907): 88–105.
51. Neppi Modona, *Carceri*, 1946–1947.

9

Conclusion

The first few years after World War I saw a renewed interest in the prison question. The positive school of criminology, led by Enrico Ferri, dominated this new reform effort and successfully asserted its ideas in a project for a new penal code. Other longstanding issues, such as the status of the prison guards and the revision of the general prison regulations, were also partially addressed according to the wishes of the positive school. As with many of the reform efforts in the liberal era, however, these too would be largely a dead letter, as the liberal era gave way to the Fascist state of Benito Mussolini.

The project for a new penal code, initiated in 1919, constituted the most ambitious reform program of the postwar period. The Royal Commission, chaired by Enrico Ferri, stated that its intent was either to revise existing penal statutes to make them more workable, or to write "a new and autonomous systemization of legislative norms in accord with the advance of scientific doctrines."[1]

In other words, Ferri and the rest of the commission fully intended to shape the project according to the ideas of criminal anthropology. This intention became crystal clear when Ferri stated that the principles of "social defense" and "the dangerousness of the offender" would inform the new code. Just as he had argued in the earlier debates on the Zanardelli penal code, Ferri demanded that society be protected from the most threatening criminals:

> Hence the fundamental criteria for a reform of laws on social defense against criminality, must be that repressive measures should be more severe . . . for habitual offenders, and those more dangerous through congenital or acquired tendency, and less rigorous . . . for the great majority of occasional offenders and those less dangerous.[2]

Furthermore, Ferri demanded that the sanctions to protect society from its criminals should not be designed to strike the conscience but rather "should provide only for the most effective social defense against dangerous offenders, and for the most rapid and sure redemption and reutilization of less dangerous offenders."[3]

The commission then offered sanctions that included indeterminate sentences, but not in cellular prisons. In other words, each offender would be segregated from honest society for as long as it took for him "to become fitted for a life of freedom." If an inmate remained dangerous and incorrigible, then the Commission maintained that he should be confined for life. The preferred location for this segregation would be agricultural colonies rather than cellular prisons because the experience of the liberal period had revealed that cellular prisons were little more than "tombs of the living." The agricultural colonies, however, were suited to Italy because many Italian offenders came from agricultural backgrounds.[4]

The commission also addressed the thorny question of prison labor. On the one hand, it asserted that work in prison was essential to prevent prisoners from leading a life of idleness and ease at the expense of honest society. On the other hand, it recognized that prison labor had constituted a threat (or perceived threat) to free workers in the liberal era. To solve this dilemma, the commission recommended that each inmate be required to perform productive and educational work, for which he would be paid a salary. The money he earned would not go into his pocket, however, but to the government for his food and clothing. Some of his salary would also be channeled to his own family and to the victims of his crime.[5]

As the first phase of this project neared completion, the prison administration began to revise the general regulations of the prisons. The overall goal was to reduce the rigidity of the *Regolamento*, thus continuing the process of revision that had begun soon after its publication in 1891. Following the lead of the positive school, the revisions changed the previously uncompromising position on cellular segregation during the first stage of imprisonment. Certain types of inmates were given the right to smoke and to pursue individual hobbies. The wages paid for prison labor were also augmented.[6]

Other reforms also occurred in the early 1920s. In response to their organized agitation and complaints, prison guards were granted better hours and working conditions.[7] An even more important reform was the transfer of the prison administration from the Ministry of the Interior to the Ministry of Justice. Begun in 1923, this transfer fulfilled a goal advocated by Lucchini and Ferri, among others, during the liberal era.[8]

These reforms proved temporary, however. The proposed project for a new penal code was scrapped in the mid-1920s. At the end of the decade, the Fascist state initiated a new era in the history of the Italian prison system. It began with the passage of a new penal code, the Alfredo Rocco Code, in 1930, and a new set of general prison regulations in 1931.[9] It continued with Mussolini's own brutal brand of criminal justice.

The liberal idea of a reformed prison system therefore met with only limited success. Yet Italian intellectuals and politicians persisted in attempts to establish a national prison system. Continued calls for prison reform generally followed the crime rate, which increased dramatically in this period. This increase sparked endless debates among reformers and politicians on how to stop or control the criminal population. Bellazzi, Beltrani-Scalia, and Turati, for example, all linked the need for prison reform to Italy's "sad primacy" in crime.

The desire to build an effective and "modern" prison system in the new nation-state transcended the simple goal of seeking to deter crime within Italy, however. Throughout the liberal era, Italian politicians and reformers clamored for a successful prison system as a symbol of great-power status. Bellazzi and Beltrani-Scalia, for example, regarded a sophisticated prison system as a measure of a nation's modernity. And Beltrani-Scalia, a regular participant in international penitentiary conferences, earnestly tried to prove that Italy could rival Britain and France in the achievements of its criminal justice institutions.

But there was a serious flaw in this kind of thinking. Italy, unlike its European rivals, was ultimately unsuited to any attempt to create a homogeneous prison system. The clear and chronic economic and social disparity between the North and the South would make it virtually impossible for any single model of criminal justice to work throughout the entire country. Persistent financial difficulties throughout this period, moreover, only exacerbated and reinforced these problems and perceptions. Yet no amount of money could have changed Italy's disparate kingdom or have led to the creation of a prison system on a truly national and integrated basis.

On the other hand, the perpetual frustration inherent in attempts to create a prison system worthy of a great power accounts for much of the appeal of the positive school. Lombroso's idea of the born criminal provided a clear rationale for abandonment of the effort to create any kind of national prison system. His proposals for agricultural colonies, moreover, seemed tailored to the anemic economy of the South and thereby offered a ready alternative to the high costs of the penitentiary.

So, in liberal Italy, while everyone was transfixed by issues of crime and punishment, no one ever formulated or implemented a viable prison system for the state as a whole. When legislation was adopted, such as the *Regolamento*, it was almost immediately thereafter revised and weakened. This kind of nagging uncertainty about both the theory and the practice of criminal justice, coupled to the kingdom's systemic economic and social problems, led to inaction and, eventually, failure. Liberal Italy's search for a reformed prison system would in the end remain an unfulfilled quest.[10]

Notes

1. Italy. Ministero della Giustizia. Commissione Reale per la Riforma delle Legge Penali istituita con R. decreto 14 settembre 1919, *Relazione sul progetto preliminare di Codice Penale Italiano* (Rome: "L'Universelle", 1921), 371.
2. Ibid., 376.
3. Ibid., 383. Ferri used the word "sanction" instead of penalty because he thought it reflected the concept of social defense. In other words, he saw it as a "reaction" by society to the "action" of the offender. See ibid., 460.
4. Ibid., 384–386. It will be recalled that Beltrani-Scalia had advocated the use of agricultural colonies for the same reasons. See chapter 4.
5. Ibid., 479–482. Ferri had long demanded that the victims of crime obtain some sort of compensation for their loss. See chapter 5.
6. Neppi Modona, *Carcere*, 1957–1958.
7. ACS, Ministero di Grazia e Giustizia, Direzione generale degli istituti di prevenzione e pena, Archivio generale, Busta 600; and Neppi Modona, *Carcere*, 1949–1954.
8. Querci-Seriacopi, *Il passato*, 67–68.
9. Neppi Modona, *Carcere*, 1966–1968.
10. This pattern of ineffective reform and paper legislation was not confined to the prison system. Mary Gibson has shown, for example, that Italy's attempts to regulate prostitution in the liberal era were persistent but ultimately ineffective. See Mary Gibson, *Prostitution and the State in Italy, 1860–1915* (New Brunswick, N.J.: Rutgers Univ. Press, 1986), especially 2–3, 224. Frank Snowden has also analyzed the ineffective response of the liberal state in the face of cholera outbreaks in Naples in 1884 and 1911. See his *Cholera in Naples* (Cambridge: Cambridge Univ. Press, 1995), especially 360–367.

Bibliography

Archival Sources

Archivio Centrale dello Stato (Rome). Presidenza del Consiglio, Gabinetto, Atti amministrativi.

————. Ministero dell'Interno, Direzione generale delle carceri e dei riformatorii, Archivio generale.

————. Ministero dell'Interno, Direzione Generale della Pubblica Sicurezza, Divisione Polizia Giudiziaria.

————. Ministero dell'Interno, Gabinetto, Rapporti dei Prefetti, 1882–1894.

————. Ministero di Grazia e Giustizia, Direzione Generale di Istituti di Prevenzione e Pena, Archivio Generale.

————. Ministero di Grazia e Giustizia, Direzione Generale di Affari Penali, Miscellanea.

————. Ministero di Grazia e Giustizia, Direzione Generale di Istituti di Prevenzione e Pena, Segreteria.

Carte di personalità

————. Carte F. Crispi, Carte A. Damiani, Carte Fambri

Newspapers

Avanti!, Rome.
Corriere della sera, Milan.
La Stampa, Turin.
Il Conciliatore.
L'Opinione, Rome.

Journals

Archivio di psichiatria, scienze penali, ed antropologia criminale
Effemeride carceraria.
Nuova Antologia.
Rivista di discipline carcerarie.
La Scuola Positiva.

Printed Primary Sources

Books

Beccaria, Cesare. *Dei delitti e delle pene.* Edited by Franco Venturi Turin: Einaudi, 1965.
Beltrani-Scalia, Martino.*La delinquenza e la statistica.*   Rome: Tip. delle Mantellate, 1888.
———. *La deportazione.* Rome: Tip. Artero e comp., 1874.
———. *La riforma carceraria in Italia.* Rome: Tip. Artero and Comp., 1879.
Caranti, Biagio. "Una colonia penitenziaria." *L'opinione* (Rome) 19 (13–16 November 1866): 1–2.
Cattaneo, Carlo. *Scritti politici.* Edited by Mario Boneschi. Florence: Felice Le Monnier, 1964.
Cerruti, Emilio. "Le colonie penali e le colonie libere." *Nuova Antologia* 23 (July 1873): 673–722.
Colajanni, Dott. Napoleone. *Ire e spropositi di Cesare Lombroso.* Catania: Filippo Tropea, 1890.
Crispi, Francesco. *Discorsi parlamentari.*   Rome: Tip. della Camera dei Deputati, 1915.
Curcio, G. *Della statistica giudiziaria civile e criminale nel Regno d'Italia.* Rome: 1873.
Curli, Guglielmo, and Sac. A. Bianchi. *Le nostre carceri e i nostri riformatori.* Milan: Enrico Rechiedei, 1902.
De Foresta, Adolfo. *Nè patibolo nè carcere.*   Bologna: Nicola Zanichelli, 1880.
Ferri, Enrico. *Criminal Sociology.* Translated by Joseph I. Kelly and John Lisle. Boston: Little, Brown, and Co., 1917.
———. *Lavoro e celle dei condannati.* Rome: Libreria Nuova, 1886.
———. *The Positive School of Criminology.* Translated by Ernest Untermann. Chicago: Charles H. Kerr and Company, 1913.
———. *Studi sulla criminalità ed altri saggi.* Turin: Fratelli Bocca, 1901.

————. *Sul nuovo codice penale: discorsi alla Camera dei Deputati*. Naples: Luigi Pierro, 1889.

Garofalo, Baron Raffaele. *Criminology*. Translated by Robert Wyness Millar. Montclair, N.J.: Patterson Smith, 1968.

Gemelli, Agostino. *Le dottrine moderne della delinquenza*. 3rd Edition. Milan: Società editrice "Vita e pensiero," 1920.

Giolitti, Giovanni. *Discorsi extraparlamentari*. Edited by Nino Valeri. Milan: Einaudi, 1952.

————. *Memoirs of My Life*. Translated by Edward Storer. New York: Howard Fertig, 1973.

Gladstone, William E. *A Letter to the Earl of Aberdeen on the State Prosecutions of the Neapolitan Government*. London: John Murray, 1851.

Howard, John. *The State of the Prisons*. New York: E. P. Dutton and Co., 1929.

Lombroso, Cesare. *Crime: Its Causes and Remedies*. Translated by Henry P. Horton. Boston: Little, Brown, and Co., 1912.

————. *Il delitto politico e le rivoluzioni*. Turin: Bocca, 1890.

————. *L'uomo delinquente in rapport all'antropologia, alla giurisprudenza ed alle discipline carcerarie*. Third Edition. Rome: Napoleone editore s.r.l., 1968.

————. *Palimsesti del carcere*. Turin: Fratelli Bocca, 1888.

————. *Sull'incremento del delito in Italia e sui mezzi per arrestarlo*. 2nd ed. Turin: Fratelli Bocca, 1879.

Lucchini, Luigi. *I semplicisti del diritto penale*. Turin: UTET, 1886.

Minghelli-Vaini, Giuseppe. *Sulla riforma delle carceri e l'assistenza pubblica*. Turin: G. Bocca, 1852.

Morichini, Carlo-Luigi. *Degli istituti di carità per la sussistenza e l'educazione dei poveri e dei prigionieri in Roma*. Rome: Stabilimento Tip. Camerale, 1870.

Paterson, Sir Alexander. *Italian Prisons: A Report of Visits to Some Italian Prisons and Reformatories in the Autumn of 1923*. Maidstone, England: H.M.C. Prison, 1924.

Peri, Carlo. *Cenni sulla riforma del sistema penitenziario in Toscana*. Florence: Società di Patrocinio , 1848.

Petitti di Roreto, Count Carlo Iliarone. *Opere scelte*. Edited by Gian Mario Bravo. Turin: Einaudi, 1969.

Prisons and Reformatories at Home and Abroad, Being the Transactions of the International Penitentiary Congress. Edited by Edwin Pears. London: Longman and Green and Co., 1872.

Settembrini, Luigi. *Ricordanze della mia vita e Scritti autobiografici*. Edited by Mario Themelly. Milan: Feltrinelli, 1961.

Turati, Filippo. *Carceri–Repressione dei tumulti e fondi*. Milan: Uffici della

Critica sociale, 1906.

———. *Il delitto e la questione sociale*. 3rd ed. Bologna: Casa editrice "La contro-corrente", 1913.

———. *Discorsi parlamentari*. Rome: Tip. della Camera dei Deputati, 1950.

Zanardelli, Giuseppe. *Discorsi parlamentari*. Rome: Tip. della Camera dei Deputati, 1905.

Italian Government Publications

Italy. Istituto centrale di statistica. *Sommario di statistiche storiche dell'Italia, 1861–1975*. Rome, 1976.

Italy. Ministero della Giustizia. Commissione Reale per la riforma delle leggi penali. *Relazione sul progetto preliminare di codice penale italiano*. Rome: "L'Universelle," 1921.

Italy. Ministero dell'Interno. Direzione generale delle carceri. *La colonizzazione interna nelle sue applicazioni col mezzo delle colonie penali agricole*. Rome: Tip. delle Mantellate, 1912.

———. *Ordinamento generale della amministrazione carceraria*. Rome: Tip. delle Mantellate, 1891.

———. *Regolamento generale degli stabilimenti carcerarii e dei riformatorii governativi*. Rome: Tip. delle Mantellate, 1891.

———. *Statistica decennale delle carceri (1870–1879)*. Civitavecchia: Tip. del Bagno Penale, 1880.

Italy. Parlamento. Camera dei Deputati and Senato. *Atti parlamentari*. Rome: Tip. della Camera dei Deputati e Tipografia del Senato.

Italy. Parlamento. Senato. *Notizie sul Senato e indice per materie degli atti del Parlamento*. Rome: Tip. del Senato, 1898.

Raccolta ufficiale delle leggi e dei decreti del Regno d'Italia. Rome: Istituto poligrafico dello Stato, 1861–1946.

Secondary Works

Alper, Benedict S., and Jerry F. Boren, *Crime : International Agenda*. Lexington, Mass.: Lexington Books, 1972.

Aquarone, Alberto. *L'unificazione legislative e i codici di 1865*. Milan: Dott. A. Giuffrè, 1960.

Babini, Valeria Paola, Maurizia Cotti, Fernanda Minuz, and Annamaria Tagliavini. *Tra sapere e potere: La psichiatria italiana nella seconda metà dell'Ottocento*. Bologna: Mulino, 1982.

Barrows, Susanna. *Distorting Mirrors: Visions of the Crowd in Late Nineteenth-Century France.* New Haven, Conn.: Yale University Press, 1981.

Belloni, Giulio Andrea. *Cattaneo criminalista.* Milan: Fratelli Bocca, 1943.

Beltrani-Scalia, Martino. *Sul governo e sulla riforma delle carceri in Italia.* Turin: Tip. G. Favale and Comp., 1867.

Bosworth, R. J. B. *Italy, the Least of the Great Powers.* London: Cambridge University Press, 1979.

Bulferetti, Luigi. *Cesare Lombroso.* Turin: UTET, 1975.

Calisse, Carlo. *A History of Italian Law.* Translated by Layton B. Register. New Jersey: Rothman Reprints, 1969.

Candeloro, Giorgio. *Storia dell'Italia moderna.* 9 vols. Milan: Feltrinelli, 1960.

Canosa, Romano. *Storia del manicomio in Italia dall'Unità ad oggi.* Milan: Feltrinelli, 1979.

Capelli, Anna. *La buona compagnia: Utopia e realtà carceraria nell'Italia del Risorgimento.* Milan: Franco Angeli, 1988.

Carocci, Giampiero. *Agostino Depretis e la politica interna italiana dal 1876 al 1887.* Turin: Einaudi, 1956.

Carpenter, Mary. *Reformatory Prison Discipline, as developed by the Rt. Hon. Walter Crofton, in the Irish Convict Prisons.* London: Longman, Longman and Green, 1872.

Castronovo, Valerio. *La stampa italiana dall'unità al fascismo.* Bari: Laterza, 1970.

Clark, Martin. *Modern Italy: 1871–1982.* London: Longman Group Ltd., 1985.

Cohen, Stanley, and Andrew Scull, eds. *Social Control and the State.* New York: St. Martin's Press, 1983.

Colombo, Giorgio. *La scienza infelice: Il museo di antropologia criminale di Cesare Lombroso.* Turin: Paolo Boringhieri, 1975.

Conti, Ugo. *La pena e il sistema penale del codice italiano.* In *Enciclopedia del diritto penale*, IV. Edited by Enrico Pessina. Milan: Società editrice libreria, 1910.

Coppa, Frank J. *Dictionary of Modern Italian History.* Westport, Conn.: Greenwood Press, 1985.

Croce, Benedetto. *A History of Italy, 1871–1915.* Translated by Cecilia M. Ady. Oxford: Clarendon Press, 1929.

Dal Canto, Pietro. *Biografia di Federico Bellazzi.* Florence: Tip. Bonducciana di C. Alessandri, 1869.

Daniels, Elizabeth Adams. *Jesse White Mario: Risorgimento Revolutionary.* Athens, Ohio: Ohio University Press, 1972.

Davis, John Anthony. *Conflict and Control: Law and Order in Nineteenth-Century Italy.* Atlantic Highlands, N.J.: Humanities Press Intl., 1987.

DeLacy, Margaret. *Prison Reform in Lancashire, 1700–1850.* Stanford: Stanford University Press, 1986.

Digesto italiano. Edited by Luigi Lucchini. Turin: UTET, 1891.

Ekirch, A. Robert. *Bound for America.* New York: Oxford University Press, 1987.

Eriksson, Torsten. *The Reformers.* New York: Elsevier, 1976.

Fink, Arthur E. *Causes of Crime: Biological Theories in the United States, 1800–1915.* Westport, Conn.: Greenwood Press, 1985.

Foerster, Robert F. *The Italian Emigration of Our Times.* Cambridge, Mass.: Harvard University Press, 1924.

Foucault, Michel. *Discipline and Punish.* Translated by Alan Sheridan. New York: Vintage, 1979.

Fried, Robert. *The Italian Prefects.* New Haven, Connecticut: Yale University Press, 1963.

Galante Garrone, Alessandro. *Felice Cavallotti.* Turin: UTET, 1976.

Garland, David. *Punishment and Modern Society.* Chicago: University of Chicago Press, 1990.

———. *Punishment and Welfare.* Vermont: Gower Pulishing Co., 1985.

Ghisalberti, Carlo. *Storia costituzionale d'Italia, 1849–1948.* Bari: Laterza, 1974.

Gibson, Mary. *Prostitution and the State in Italy, 1860–1915.* New Brunswick, New Jersey: Rutgers University Press, 1986.

Gildemeister, Glen A. *Prison Labor and Contract Competition with Workers in Industrializing America, 1840–1890.* New York: Garland Publishing Co., 1987.

Gillin, John Lewis. *Criminology and Penology.* New York: D. Appleton-Century, Co., 1935.

Gooch, John. *Army, State, and Society in Italy, 1870–1915.* New York: St. Martin's Press, 1989.

Gould, Stephen Jay. *The Mismeasure of Man.* New York: Norton, 1978.

———. *Ontogeny and Phylogeny.* Cambridge, Mass.: Belknap Press, 1977.

Greenfield, Kent Roberts. *Economics and Liberalism in the Risorgimento.* 2nd ed. Baltimore: Johns Hopkins University Press, 1965.

Gregor, A. James. *Young Mussolini and the Intellectual Origins of Fascism.* Berkeley: University of California Press, 1979.

Griffiths, Major Arthur. *Italian Prisons: St. Angelo—The Piombi—The Vicaria—Prisons of the Roman Inquisition.* London: The Grolier Society, 1890.

Grillandi, Massimo. *Francesco Crispi.* Turin: UTET, 1969.

Harris, Ruth. *Murders and Madness.* Cambridge, England: Cambridge University Press, 1989.

Hearder, Harry. *Italy in the Age of the Risorgimento, 1790–1860*. London: Longman Group Ltd., 1983.

Ignatieff, Michael. *A Just Measure of Pain*. New York: Pantheon, 1978.

Jensen, Richard Bach. "Liberty and Order: The Theory and Practice of Italian Public Security Policy, 1848 to the Crisis of the 1890s." Ph.D. diss., University of Minnesota, 1982.

Kurella, Hans. *Cesare Lombroso: A Modern Man of Science*. Translated by M. Eden Paul. New York: Rebman Co., 1910.

Lindesmith, Alfred, and Yale Levin. "The Lombrosian Myth in Criminology." *American Journal of Sociology* 42 (July 1936- May 1937): 653–671.

Lombroso-Ferrero, Gina. *Cesare Lombroso: storia della vita e delle opere*. 2nd ed. Bologna: Nicola Zanichelli, 1921.

———. *Criminal Man According to the Classification of Cesare Lombroso*. Montclair, N. J.: Patterson Smith, 1972.

Lovett, Clara. *Carlo Cattaneo and the Politics of the Risorgimento*. The Hague: Martinus Nijhoff, 1972.

Mack Smith, Denis. *Italy: A Modern History*. New Edition, Revised and Expanded. Ann Arbor: University of Michigan Press, 1969.

Maestro, Marcello. *Cesare Beccaria and the Origins of Penal Reform*. Philadelphia: Temple University Press, 1965.

Mandracci, Vera Comoli, and Giovanni Maria Lupo. *Il carcere giudiziario di Torino detto "Le Nuove"*. Turin: Centro Studi Piemontesi, 1974.

Mannheim, Hermann, ed. *Pioneers in Criminology*. Chicago: Quadrangle Books, Inc., 1960.

Matthew, H. C. G. *Gladstone, 1809–1874*. Oxford: Clarendon Press, 1986.

Melossi, Dario, and Massimo Pavarini. *The Prison and the Factory*. Translated by Glynis Cousin. Totowa, N. J.: Barnes and Noble, 1981.

Molfese, Franco. *Storia del brigantaggio dopo l'Unità*. Milan: Feltrinelli, 1964.

Mosse, George L. *Toward the Final Solution: A History of European Racism*. New York: Howard Fertig, 1978.

Navarra, Antonietta. *La edilizia carceraria*. Naples: Libreria Scientifica Ed., 1967.

Neppi Modona, Guido. "Carceri e società civile." In *Storia d'Italia*, 5 (2), 1909–1998. Turin: Einaudi, 1973.

Nye, Robert A. *Crime, Madness, and Politics in Modern France*. Princeton: Princeton University Press, 1985.

———. "Heredity or Milieu: The Foundations of Modern European Criminological Theory." *Isis* 67 (1976): 335–356.

O'Brien, Patricia. "Crime and Punishment as Historical Problem." *Journal of Social History* (1978): 508–520.

————. *The Promise of Punishment: Prisons in Nineteenth-Century France*. Princeton: Princeton University Press, 1982.

Pancaldi, Giuliano. *Darwin in Italia*. Bologna: Mulino, 1983.

Perrot, Michelle, ed. *L'impossible prison*. Paris: Editions du Seuil, 1971.

Pessina, Enrico. *Il diritto penale in Italia da Cesare Beccaria sino alla promulgazione del codice penale vigente*. In *Enciclopedia del diritto penale italiano*. Edited by Enrico Pessina. Milan: Società Editrice Libraria, 1906.

Phillipson, Coleman. *Three Criminal Law Reformers*. Montclair, N.J.: Patterson Smith, 1970.

Pick, Daniel. *Faces of Degeneration*. Cambridge, England: Cambridge University Press, 1989.

Pirovano, Carlo, ed. *Modern Italy: Images and History of a National Identity*. Milan: Electa Editrice, 1982.

Priestly, Philip. *Victorian Prison Lives*. London: Methuen, 1985.

Procacci, Giuliano. *History of the Italian People*. Translated by Anthony Paul. London: Penguin, 1970.

Querci-Seriacopi, Ernesto. *Il passato, il presente, e l'avvento dell'amministrazione delle carceri in Italia*. Rome: Tip. delle Mantellate, 1925.

Renda, Francesco. *I fasci siciliani, 1892–1894*. Turin: Einaudi, 1977.

Rennie, Isabel. *The Search for Criminal Man*. Lexington, Mass.: Lexington Books, 1978.

Romanelli, Raffaele. *L'Italia liberale (1868–1900)*. Bologna: Mulino, 1979.

Rothman, David. *The Discovery of the Asylum*. Boston: Little, Brown, and Co., 1971.

Ruck, S. K., ed. *Paterson on Prisons: Being the Collected Papers of Sir Alexander Paterson*. London: Frederick Muller, Ltd., 1951.

Salomone, A. William. *Italy in the Giolittian Era*. Philadelphia: University of Pennsylvania Press, 1941.

Scarabello, Giovanni. *Carcerati e carceri a Venezia nell'età moderna*. Rome: Istituto della Enciclopedia Italiana, 1979.

Sellin, Thorsten. "A New Phase of Criminal Anthropology in Italy." *Annals of the American Academy* 125–126 (1926): 233–242.

Seton-Watson, Christopher. *Italy from Liberalism to Fascism, 1870–1925*. London: Methuen, 1967.

Shannon, Richard. *Gladstone*. London: Hamish Hamilton, 1982.

Smith, Beverly A. "The Irish Prison System, 1854–1914: Prisons and Political Prisoners." Ph.D. diss., Miami University, Ohio, 1982.

Snowden, Frank. *Cholera in Naples*. Cambridge: Cambridge University Press,

1995.

Spirito, Ugo. *Storia del diritto penale italiano da Cesare Beccaria ai nostri giorni.* Florence: G. C. Sansoni, 1974.

Sylvester, Sawyer F., Jr. *The Heritage of Modern Criminology.* Cambridge, Mass.: Schenkman Publishing Company, 1972.

Thayer, John A. *Italy and the Great War: Politics and Culture, 1870–1915.* Madison, Wisconsin: University of Wisconsin Press, 1964.

Valeri, Nino. *Giovanni Giolitti.* Turin: UTET, 1972.

Venturi, Franco. *Settecento riformatore.* Turin: Einaudi, 1969.

Villa, Renzo. *Il deviante e i suoi segni.* Milan: Franco Angeli, 1985.

Woolf, Stuart. *A History of Italy, 1700–1860: The Social Constraints of Political Change.* London: Methuen, 1979.

Wright, Gordon. *Between the Guillotine and Liberty.* New York: Oxford University Press, 1983.

Yablonsky, Lewis. *Criminology.* 4th ed. New York: Harper and Row, 1990.

Zehr, Howard. *Crime and the Development of Modern Society* London: Croom Helm, 1975.

Index

Topinard, Paul, 62
torture, 15
transportation, 27, 37–40, 48 n. 2
Tre Fontane, 45, 46, 57, 105, 107
Troppo presto, 74
Tumminelli, Agostino, 47
Turati, Filippo, 3, 61, 98,
    111–112, 114
Tuscan Penal Code (1853), 26

Umberto I (king of Italy), 41, 47,
    78, 98, 114

Vacca, 26
Vazio, Napoleone, 31–32
Verri, Pietro, 7
Victor Emmanuel II (king of
    Italy), 23, 33 n. 1
Vilella, 54
Volpicella, Ferdinando,16, 20 n.
    49
Voltaire, 8

White Mario, Jesse, 94, 49 n. 25
Wright, Gordon, 2

Zanardelli Code. *See* Italian
    Criminal Law Code (1889)
Zanardelli, Giuseppe, 4, 73, 78
Zerbaglio, Adolfo, 94

Studies in Modern European History

The monographs in this series focus upon aspects of the political, social, economic, cultural, and religious history of Europe from the Renaissance to the present. Emphasis is placed on the states of Western Europe, especially Great Britain, France, Italy, and Germany. While some of the volumes treat internal developments, others deal with movements such as liberalism, socialism, and industrialization which transcend a particular country.

The series editor is:

Frank J. Coppa
Director, Doctor of Arts Program
in Modern World History
Department of History
St. John's University
Jamaica, New York 11439